DEVELOPING ENGLIS

Open University Press

English, Language, and Education series

General Editor: Anthony Adams

Lecturer in Education, University of Cambridge

This series is concerned with all aspects of language in education
from the primary school to the tertiary sector. Its authors are
experienced educators who examine both principles and practice of
English subject teaching and language across the curriculum in the
context of current educational and societal developments.

TITLES IN THE SERIES

DEVELOPING ENGLISH

EDITED BY
Peter Dougill

Open University Press
Milton Keynes · Philadelphia

Open University Press
Celtic Court
22 Ballmoor
Buckingham
MK18 1XW

and
1900 Frost Road, Suite 101
Bristol, PA 19007, USA

First published 1991

British Library Cataloguing in Publication Data

Developing English. – (English, language and education
   series).
   1. Great Britain. Primary schools. Curriculum subjects:
   English language. Teaching
   I. Dougill, Peter   II. Series
   372.60440941

   ISBN 0-335-09584-4

Library of Congress Cataloging-in-Publication Data

Developing English / edited by Peter Dougill.
      p.   cm. – (English, language, and education series)
   Includes bibliographical references (p.   )
   Includes index.
   ISBN 0-335-09584-4
   1. English philology – Study and teaching.   I. Dougill, Peter.
II. Series.
PE65.D48 1990
428′.0071′073 – dc20   90-7634
                                                        CIP

Typeset by Rowland Phototypesetting Limited
Bury St Edmunds, Suffolk
Printed in Great Britain by Biddles Limited
Guildford and King's Lynn

Contents

Learning stamps you with its moments. Childhood's learning is made up of moments. It isn't steady. It's a pulse.

Eudora Welty

List of contributors

David Allen is an English inspector in Nottinghamshire LEA and chairs the National Association for Advisers in English. He is the author of *English, Whose English?* and a number of other publications.

Alan Howe had taught in schools in the UK and Australia and was the director of the Wiltshire oracy project. His publications include *Expanding Horizons* (NATE 1988).

Ken Wilby has been head of English at Boundstone Community College, Lancing and an oracy project coordinator. He is now an English inspector in Hampshire.

Nicholas Roberts has taught in comprehensive schools in West Sussex and is currently an advisory teacher for English and language development with a particular interest in media education and information technology.

Terry Furlong is a prominent member of NATE who has lectured and written on a wide variety of English topics. Formerly English adviser in Brent he is currently seconded to work on the development of assessment strategies for the national curriculum.

Chris Marshall is an advisory teacher for English and language development in West Sussex. Formerly he was head of English at Thomas Bennett Community College, Crawley.

Nikki Siegen-Smith was a contributor to Southern Conference on knowledge about language and is headteacher of the Wilson Primary School, Reading.

Paul Rhodes was also a contributor to Southern Conference work on knowledge about language and is head of English at the Princess Margaret Royal Free School, Windsor.

Philip Pullman is a teacher, freelance writer and lecturer. In addition to *The Ruby in the Smoke* he has written a number of books and scripts including the TV serial *How to be Cool*.

Pat D'Arcy has written and lectured widely on issues concerned with writing development both in the UK and overseas. Currently she is English adviser in Wiltshire.

Sue Hackman has worked in a number of schools and colleges and is the author of books on media education and writing including *Responding in Writing* (NATE 1987). She is currently an advisory teacher in Surrey.

Nick Jones is a coordinator of the Language in the National Curriculum Project in the south-west of England. Formerly he was head of English at Bosworth College, Leicester and then English adviser in Devon.

Bronwyn Cadle is head of English at Thomas Bennett Community College, Crawley.

Jack Ousbey has taught in primary and secondary schools and until recently was a senior inspector of schools in Nottinghamshire. Now he is a freelance lecturer and writer.

Pam Barnard has been closely involved with NATE for a number of years and is currently teaching English at the Exeter tertiary college.

Dot Froggatt is currently a primary advisory headteacher. Formerly she taught at Chesworth Junior School, Horsham.

Acknowledgements

Without the help of the following this book could not have been written:

Paul Baker
John Taylor HMI
Julie Warne
Kate Marron
and the many teachers and advisers who have contributed to the work of the
Southern Conference for Development Work in English.

General editor's introduction

When this book was first proposed to me for this series I was attracted mainly by the possibility of a book growing out of the Southern Regional Conference, which I had had the honour of addressing on two occasions. This long standing annual meeting of theorists, local advisers, HMI and teachers working together in the region seemed (and still seems) to me an excellent model for continuing in-service work in English. Peter Dougill's idea was to bring together a number of the recently presented talks to the conference and some of their outcomes in terms of classroom work as described in case studies presented by individual teachers from the region. The present volume provides the final outcome.

This has led to a remarkable combination of talents. Many of the contributors to major chapters in the book are likely to be already well known to its readers. Most of the teacher contributors are unlikely (as yet anyway) to be known outside the region. However, it seems to me that this combination breaks new ground both in in-service work and its outcomes in important respects. It shows ways in which the theory and practice of English teaching can be brought very closely together. The authors of the case studies went away from their annual conference inspired to try out new things in their classrooms and sustained, in many cases, by those who had presented some of the theoretical positions to them in the first place. This gives the lie to the often advanced and, in my view, mistaken, proposition that there is a dichotomy between 'theory' and 'practice' so that the two need never meet. (Indeed I think the originally proposed title of the book was *Theory into Practice* and it is one that in many ways I am sorry to have lost.)

However, the present title is, without doubt, the correct one. We are post-Kingman, post-Cox, and (at the time of writing) awaiting Statutory Orders for English in the National Curriculum. Overseas readers may find this extra-ordinary but it is a fact that, until the Education Act of 1988, there has been no compulsory curriculum in England and Wales. The introduction of a compulsory curriculum on a statutory basis marks a complete change in the philosophy of dealing with curriculum issues. In this sense English (like other key subjects) is 'developing' at the present time and it is good to see so many of the contributors to this book anchoring their arguments so firmly (even if not always with complete agreement) to the issues raised in the key reports that have shaped the way in which the English curriculum is likely to emerge in practice.

The other major development at present is the move to local management of schools (LMS). This means that schools will be working out, to a large extent, their own priorities for their own in-service programmes (buying in help as it is seen to be needed) and much such work will be school based. While there are some virtues in this (it has been all too easy for in-service work to seem remote from the classroom), the danger is that schools will become too inward looking, too much concerned with local issues, and local problems and solutions, to be able to see things in the wider perspective. The power of the Southern Regional Conference to draw upon a national repertoire of speakers, to enable teachers to meet together on a regular basis but free from the immediate constraints of their more parochial situation, and to provide, through the advisory services, for sustaining the work of the classroom when the members had returned to the school, has been very great indeed.

Its fruits can be seen, in part at least, in this book. The rest can be seen in the work that has been done in the classrooms. One fears that with LMS such fruits may be under threat.

Anthony Adams

Introduction

The title *Developing English* is intended to indicate at least two kinds of movement. The first suggests possible shifts in the stance of those involved with the teaching of English in the 1990s. These shifts have been made more explicit through the deliberations of a sequence of working parties ranging from the Committee of Inquiry into the Teaching of English chaired by Sir John Kingman to the National Curriculum English Working Group chaired by Professor Brian Cox coupled with subsequent interventions and adjustments made by the National Curriculum Council and the DES. These various groups have drawn upon the expertise of classroom teachers which in turn has been represented by such bodies as NATE or through the work of the two national projects which have concentrated on written and spoken language. In short, there has been a tradition of reflection and development in English which has been codified by the national curriculum. If Kingman, Cox, and the national curriculum have not actually invented good practice but rather have drawn upon an existing and growing reservoir of good practice they have, nevertheless, highlighted gaps and possible weaknesses.

However, *Developing English* is not intended to be a Baedeker for use while travelling through the intricate delta of attainment targets and programmes of study. Neither does it pretend that the national curriculum is a passing fancy. Instead, it is intended to help teachers of English locate their own positions in order that they might start to accommodate the demands of national curriculum while at the same time retaining what they consider is important and what stamps them with a particular identity as teachers.

In order to attempt this the book has been organized so that movement from theory to practice is also suggested. Keynote theoretical chapters are linked to case studies which describe how these ideas have been implemented in classrooms.

As David Allen says in the opening chapter, 'there has never been a more important time to evaluate the curriculum in the classroom and the whole management of that by the department.' In one sense the chapters which follow

David Allen's are all intended to be evaluative; consequently this is the only chapter which is not paired with a case study. It is hoped that the material which follows will generate the kind of questions which may help to support English departments at a time when they are increasingly pressed not only to say what they do but why they do it.

Much, but not all, of the work represented here has come out of the Southern Conference for Development Work in English, a loosely knit group involving a number of LEAs in a form of collaborative in-service training which has allowed teachers, advisers, HMI and teacher trainers to work closely together over a number of years.

PART ONE
Evaluation

1 Evaluating the English department

DAVID ALLEN

There are plenty of bullets flying about just now. It is difficult to preserve the detachment necessary to review one's own work calmly when there are bullets flying overhead. The media and other opinion formers are enjoying the snipe season. It is altogether understandable that teachers should keep their heads down. But not very useful. The only advantage to an ostrich when it buries its head in the sand is that it limits the choice of where precisely it is shot. It will probably not be in the head.

Not that much has changed. Of all teachers, English teachers are still among the most resistant to the very idea of evaluation and accountability. Perhaps the dangers of narrowness are too well understood. Perhaps, too, they fear that the flame of art at the centre of the best of English will be so easily snuffed out by mechanical processes. If English is indeed about growth (how can it not be?), about imagination, about cultural recreation, will it wilt under rough mechanical treatment? Certainly we cannot insert evaluation into lifeless soil and expect to see new growth. A worthwhile English curriculum does not start with evaluation. It should come out of an attempt to create an experience of some merit and should in turn enhance new forms by providing evidence of effectiveness or failure. It might also help to clarify the purposes of the enterprise. It is part of the process, not its end. If evaluation is applied to the lifeless body of an inarticulate curriculum, it is really a post mortem (which is one kind of evaluation, I suppose). It may identify the fact of death; it is not much use in creating further life.

The central role of evaluation is in generating renewal and refreshment in cycle after cycle; the alternative is an unexercised atrophy, a hardening of the arteries. Evaluation can be a process that supports the living learning of children and teachers and it needs a structure that is sensitive but strong enough to provide hard information. Now, more than ever, we need a means of supporting good work by evidence rather than assertion against the many calls for reduction, for compliance, for obedience. Now, more than ever, we need evidence to keep the pointless, the ineffective, the dead, out of the classroom.

English teachers have long been able to pride themselves on the energy and liveliness of the best of their teaching. In the last twenty years or so great efforts have gone into the planning of courses and resources. But on what evidence of success or failure has the course been continued or changed? English teachers often say that they are not happy presenting the same material year after year, following the same lines. But how are the changes made? Are they on the grounds of personal taste or of ineffectiveness? How much notice is taken of the most vociferous of reaction from pupils? How much notice should be taken? Is the sense of novelty for the teacher to carry more weight than the benefit to the learner? Is the rhetoric that engaging the personal taste of the teacher makes for positive lessons so overridingly central that there are no occasions when the teacher should continue with effective material in spite of personal preference? Are there no occasions when teachers should abandon lesson methods and material they personally find attractive because the evidence, when collected and heeded, would point to unwanted effects and a need to change? The grounds for continuity or change surely need careful weighing. This is the role of evaluation or review.

Now that many of the traditional choices of the teacher are being taken away by the centralization of the national curriculum, some are saying that there is no longer any need for evaluation. Teachers are to be told in detail what to do. They are to be no more than 'classroom learning implementation operatives'. Certainly the government intends to pick up the praise if the changes lead to improvement. Only the brickbats and the work are left for the teachers to pick up. Whose work are we now evaluating?

I believe there has never been a more important time to evaluate the curriculum in the classroom and the whole management of that by the department. Many parts of the national curriculum have never been examined in practice in any systematic way and are still suspect until proved. Many kinds of good work are excluded and need to be reconsidered for inclusion as the curriculum is reviewed – as all bodies agree it must be.

There have always been good reasons to be wary of the drive to make English teaching accountable. A major one is that we may be held accountable on grounds that are unacceptable to us and run counter to the lessons learned in the classrooms where the curriculum has to be delivered. There is plenty of crass, uninformed, not to say ignorant, commentary available weekly from the media, politicians and even some parents. There are times when the kind of remarks passed provokes stunned disbelief in teachers. It is as if all the experience of working with children in classrooms is to count for nothing. How can common ground be discovered?

The common ground has to be the educational welfare of children. And one of the most profitable ways of working on this common ground has to be through the consideration of evidence collected while evaluating work in progress.

A second reason for wariness is the reluctance to have our uncertainties and inconsistencies brought out into the light, whether ours or someone else's. It is an essential characteristic of any teacher of integrity that there are doubts to live with, and an endless and unclosing gap between hopes and actualities. The national curriculum is not going to close the gap. Whoever sets the agenda there is always so much more to do. The danger is that whoever confesses first to failure may well be first to be criticized. Accountability exposes our own performance to those who do not have to live with the need for gradual development, with the job of getting the best out of a rather varied bunch of teachers (some of whom never asked to be English teachers). We have quite enough difficulty with our own honest sense of failure without handing ammunition to others.

Yet the essential difficulty of the enterprise has to be conveyed. The emptiness of so many of the simpler suggestions offered to us has to be challenged by evidence; assertion and passion no longer win arguments.

By their works shall ye know them

Even if, as I believe, evaluation has a place in the work of any English department, it is far from being the totality. Though we are a long way from overevaluating English, there is still the danger of overrating evaluation. It could become a way of life, so frantic and self-enclosing that there is no time to think about other things. Analysis to paralysis. It is not the central activity of teaching, nor is it valuable in its own right. It is only worth house- or headroom if it contributes to the quality of what children receive. It needs to be kept in perspective. A fisherman in *Aran Islands* was giving sound advice about evaluation when he said:

> A man who is not afraid of the sea will be soon be drowned for he will be going out on a day he should not. But we do be afraid of the sea and we do only be drowned now and again.

Properly understood, evaluation can prevent us going out on a day we should not. Misunderstood, drowning will be a frequent occurrence.

On the other hand, a character in one of Russell Hoban's books reminds us that 'Explorers have to be ready to die lost.' It is difficult to see how evaluation that asks real questions is to avoid being risky.

If evaluation is worthwhile it is not without its pitfalls. As such, it partakes of the qualities of learning.

1 It is a twoway process rather than a oneway transmission.
2 It seeks answers to real questions, rather than pseudo-questions.
3 It is a process that has to adapt itself to local needs and circumstances.
4 It is just as much process as product, product as process. A badly designed process will spoil the outcome and a misconceived product will sour the experience.
5 The experience of doing it teaches more than any amount of advice and dummy-run practice.

What is to be evaluated?

There are a number of possible targets for evaluation in the work of any English department. These can be broadly categorized as follows:

1 the curriculum;
2 the roles and tasks that are carried out by members of the department;
3 the costs and effects of deploying resources.

Schools are centrally concerned with the curriculum: it is their reason for existing. All else is in the service or the thwarting of that central drive. The curriculum consists of experiences believed to be worthwhile and from which learning flows. The English curriculum has not remained constant in nature or extent. Blink and something new is added, usually at the behest of the teachers themselves as they see more and more the need to connect and as they become clearer and clearer about the damage done by an oversharp carving of the learning cake. That expansion of English calls to mind what Brendan Behan said about Canada . . . 'It will be nice when it's finished.'

We can distinguish in broad terms three forms of the curriculum:

1 the intended;
2 the received;
3 the entitlement.

We all mean well but there will always be a gap between what we intend and what we do. Nevertheless, any department intends to provide a good learning experience. The question is, what do the children actually receive? It is what they understand or what they experience that influences their learning. No amount of goodwill can compensate for a course that is taken amiss by the recipients. It is when the intent and the reception are in concert that a department can begin to make inroads into the entitlement that every child has. The idea of the 'entitlement' curriculum is that every child has a right of access to a whole range of valuable learning experiences and that this cannot be left to accident. Entitlement has a resounding rhetoric but a cracked reality if that reciprocality has not been established. Part of the thrust behind the national curriculum has been the need to establish the features of an education for all. But specifying the design features is not enough; there must also be an evaluation for their reception in practice.

In presenting a case for evaluation, I must obviously put the case for a worthwhile curriculum. One way of presenting one example for consideration might be through a series of underpinning key statements, which seek to exemplify the entitlement and which, if they came to reality, would add up to a rich, broad, learning experience. As such they might be seen as a collection of little manifestos, based on the lessons of classroom experience and on a wide reading in the literature of learning and language development. The ones that follow were created originally to indicate where a department was going; 'if you do not know where you are going, you will probably end up somewhere else'.

Towards a satisfactory English programme

Language and learning

1.1 Language is both a medium of learning and a matter for learning – and children learn by behaving like successful language users, reflecting on what they have done.

1.2 How children learn is more important than what they learn at any one time, though the quality of what they learn through cannot be left to chance. *How* we teach is of more enduring import than *what* we teach.

1.3 All learning is enhanced by reflection on the experience – the how and the why – at all ages.

1.4 Learning has the same characteristics at every age. Thus teachers need to reflect, as a professional matter, on their own ways with words.

1.5 Language develops incrementally by an interaction between the four modes of listening, talking, reading and writing. Any course should promote this interaction in a positive way by a planned flow from one mode to another.

1.6 We learn by doing what we want to learn, not by preparing for it or by artificial practice of subskills.

1.7 Story is one of the fundamental means of thinking, a deep pattern of the brain – so story should be experienced in every language mode.

1.8 Awareness typically develops when something gives us pause and when consequently, instead of just acting, we stop to consider the possibilities of acting that are before us. The claim is that we heighten our awareness of what is actual by considering what is possible. We are conscious of what we do to the extent that we are conscious also of we do *not* do – of what we might have done. The notion of choice is thus central.

(Margaret Donaldson)[1]

Reading

2.1 Children learn to read by behaving like readers and reflecting on what they do.

2.2 Books teach children to read, so there must be a lot of quality books easily accessible. Both children and teachers need hands-on experience. Children are entitled to exercise choice in the realm of reading.

2.3 Reading is caught like measles, and you cannot pass it on unless you carry the virus. It is a prime function of a school, not a peripheral one, to spread the virus of voluntary reading.

2.4 'Effective reading is the willingness to reflect on what is read' (Keith Gardner).[2]

2.5 Teachers need to be seen as real readers, reading, enthusing, disliking, showing preferences and explaining them.

2.6 All readers need help in deepening their understanding of what they have read. This is not gained by answering other people's questions, but by increasing the range of one's own.

2.7 Reading and sharing poetry should be a regular and normal activity if it is to be seen as normal. It cannot be postponed until a later teacher.

2.8 The shared class reader has a place in any classroom but it does not suffice as a reading course in itself.

2.9 The entitlement reading experience makes room for a range and balance of all kinds of reading – fiction, fact, poetry, journalism, short, long, – for a whole range of purposes.

2.10 Reading teaches reading, but reading with active discussion and lively writing teaches it better.

2.11 Professional ('real') writers should be a normal part of school life. They 'speak' of the nature of writing.

Writing

3.1 Writing begins as it ends – with speaking to oneself. That is its connection with thinking. It is not a means of demonstrating what the writer cannot do. The child writer should be seen in this positive way.

3.2 Meaning is what matters, more than anything, and the teacher's response should always be to the message first.

3.3 The audience disciplines the writer and children should experience the pressures of a variety of audiences.

3.4 Writing teaches writing, but writing preceded by vigorous discussion and reading of quality will teach it better.

3.5 It is the only function of teacher response to help the child to develop as a writer. Children should be helped to affect the response that they are given rather than merely accepting it.

3.6 It is vital to prove to children that they are succeeding. That is the growth point and the platform to greater effort.

3.7 There should be a regular opportunity to redraft and polish (which is not the same as writing out a neat version). There should be regular opportunity to decide that a piece does not warrant reworking. Some writing should be given time and scope to develop at length.

3.8 The teacher must be seen as a writer, since she is the nearest model they have. There must be time to share writing with the children and to be explicit about the difficulty, the inherent failure to say exactly what one means.

3.9 Some knowledge about language seems to be worth making explicit – such as the influence of audience, or ways of handling the requirements of particular kinds of writing. These are concerned with how language varies from context to context, or with crafting techniques. There seems to be no equivalent value in the explicit analysis of the internal organs of the sentence and none whatsoever in the naming of those organs.

Talking and listening

4.1 'My talk is the pen of a ready writer' (*The Book of Common Prayer*).

4.2 To develop as talkers children must be given time to talk and reason to listen. It is not the purpose of that time to undermine their confidence in their own language. To undermine confidence is to hinder development. It is antipathetic to the aim of developing oracy to attempt to ridicule or demean the speaker.

4.3 There has to be scope for many different kinds of talk and many different purposes. Audience and purpose put pressure on the point of utterance. Story telling, opinion, problem solving, planning, questioning, instructing, discussing, asserting, lecturing . . . The central ones are those that take place in the small group.

4.4 Drama has a central and irreplaceable role in language development. It cannot be seen as an option.

4.5 Good talk is stimulated by good reading, talking, listening, writing and lively direct experience. They will also give good reason for effective listening.

4.6 The teacher is one of the best (or worst) models of speaker and listener that the children have and is most effective as a partner in an enterprise: the model of talking 'as teacher' is of little use to children.

Continuity and entitlement

5.1 Each child has the right to encounter a broad range of activities and language demands.

5.2 Each language activity has its strengths and its limitations. Some lose their value very quickly and fade if repeated. Others need to be experienced frequently to give their full value. This argues a need to plan an appropriate frequency for each activity if the best is to be offered.

This is a far from complete framework for a halfway decent English course; but it is far better than many that are operating in classrooms at this minute. The limitations of the framework were made all the clearer in the act of constructing it. Yet it offered, when put forward, an attempt at sufficient complexity and at coherence in a little compass. It represented an ambition worth the attempt. It was meant to serve as a short but dense focus for the work of an English department. It stood for a minimum guaranteed richness, since the idea behind it was that whatever was included was the unwavering determination of every member of the department and the entitlement of every child. It represented an agreement not to opt out, not to leave it to others.

There are times when the received curriculum is like a game of pinball, in which the child is fired at speed towards the curriculum and bounces off the personal enthusiasms of each teacher. Whether the sum total of such enthusiasm adds up to a worthwhile education I have come to doubt, when major elements are left to chance.

The statements offered above seek to describe an entitlement. They have a number of underpinning assumptions:

1 Whatever is included is for all children.
2 It is the experience that teaches.
3 Each experience has its gifts and its limitations.
4 A broad range of experiences is a move 'forwards to basics'.
5 Learning is holistic, not a mounting collection of sub-skills separately acquired and deployed.

These assumptions are not universally held, either within the teaching profession or in the population at large. Take the teacher who said that he did not promote much discussion in his classroom because the children he taught were not very articulate. Or the teacher who only allowed one piece of writing per term because he had found that the more the children wrote the more their spelling 'went to pot'.

The view we take of learning must be ambitious for the children. It must also relate to the evidence from practice. It has to be rooted in the ends that we have in our educational sights. Education is both an effective means and a valuable end. The curriculum advanced in any advocacy will be seen by the advocate as both an experience of quality and a means to a life of quality. There is no such thing as a value free view of education. The values implicit in the curriculum described above are, or should be, transparent to anyone.

Some English teachers still believe in the 'coffee cup' curriculum and evaluation. All the necessary planning and evaluation, it would seem, can be carried out over break with a well deserved cup of coffee. That hardly amounts to a prolonged or searching look. It is clear that in the snatch of conversation at such times there is no chance for any more than a brief reinforcement of sanity and systems maintenance. (Did you have much trouble with Wayne last year? Have you got the other fifteen copies of X? Have you got that extract that you mentioned last week?) Such matters do have to be sorted. And there are positive ways of using those snatched moments. In the nature of things they are best used for alerting, checking, pushing on. Thus a new topic can be opened up for later discussion, worries can be aired, matters decided at the last meeting can be chased, practical help can be given, praise and interest dispensed . . .

However, such short encounters are no substitute for a prolonged look at some part of the curriculum, nor for a searching look at the best ways of implementing the national curriculum and getting the best out of it; or preventing the worst damage. There will be many teachers who are driven by anxiety and isolation to take the mechanical way out. This will not be the best way for children. Nor will it be the best way for that teacher, for it will sell the death of professionalism and the end of a learning posture, which is the only way to stay interested in teaching. That learning posture is another of the characteristics of a self-evaluating department.

The assumptions behind the 'coffee cup' curriculum are:

1 that the curriculum is a collection of individual bits;
2 that it is brought ready made by all who are trained;
3 that it is so simple that it can be absorbed in gobbets and assembled in the head;
4 that excellence is accidental and idiosyncratic.

The contrary view, advanced here, is that the simple curriculum is likely to be a bad one, that the 'coffee cup' curriculum is likely to be reductive, disparate, contradictory, omitting essentials and entitlements. Further, the 'coffee cup' evaluation will probably pay more attention to initial pupil reaction, whether for or against, than to evidence of learning, which requires a longer, cooler look. Coherence and impact both have to be worked on in collaboration. The English department should be a city state rather than an archipelago.

In deciding suitable targets for evaluation a department would obviously look at its own agenda. However, there are a number of candidates in most departments that would benefit from a consideration of how they are perceived by the children and a detached look at the messages they often inadvertently give about learning. Though no one ever intends to say so, the message put over about reading is often, 'You will understand more of what you read if I test what you do not understand about the last piece. In doing so, I shall not use your questions but someone else's.' What over a period of time does that teach about the place of reading in children's lives?

Similarly, how often in responding to a child's writing does a teacher give the message, 'I do not care what you mean; I shall seek out and show you the mistakes you have made.' Again, there are deep and lasting effects on learning from that response over a period of time. The teacher needs to look back and see what the cumulative message has been. It may be very different to what was intended.

Reading occupies a substantial part of English lessons. The overt messages are clear and positive. But what about the subliminal messages? 'I read out the bits I think are important and interesting, from a book I choose, at a time that I choose, for as long as I think suitable.' Does reading not become something owned by others and carried out at their request? Yet no adult reader operates like that. There are clear implications for the reading curriculum here.

We all want talk in the classroom and great ingenuity goes into constructing group activities. However, there is an approach endemic to groupwork in many classrooms which, whether the teacher wishes or not, gives a very consistent lesson about talk. 'I want you to talk on my topic, in the way I want. Before you have got very far, I shall come around to your group and stop what you are doing to see how far you have got. While I am with you, I shall give you some of my ideas which are better than yours, because it is my task and I have been thinking about it longer than you have.' Again, no one means to say this, but the meaning of the actions is much more powerful than the intention, particularly when they are repeated in a routine way. Only dispassionate observation and reflection can reveal the accuracy or otherwise of this analysis in any particular classroom.

There are many such areas of the curriculum where the message of our actions is not in tune with our rhetoric. There are very powerful effects on the learning of children and they often completely subvert all our good words. To tread here requires a department approach rather than an exploration alone. It also requires a confidence born of sound foundations and evidence of success.

Starting the account in the black – the self-evaluating department

The word evaluation carries overtones to many people of fault finding and carping. It is important for a department to start with a more positive frame of mind. Wherever one looks there is work of some quality. Evaluation should start with a profile of achievement, carefully and scrupulously done. This will seem to many a peculiar occupation. Yet it recognizes a central fact of learning – success leads the learner on more energetically into the areas of doubt and dispute. It also engenders a more balanced view of one's failures. It is essential in all learning to have a sense of perspective. What I am talking about here is not the easy collection of platitudes but a searching, challenging enquiry into success.

Any ingrained evaluation should make room for a regular collection of good things, because morale is important: it draws people together in a common pursuit; it strengthens the department for the encounter with unfairness, with disappointment. This same concentration on the positives in the first stages should also characterize the evaluation of roles and tasks in the department.

Before any work is done, it would be as well to bear in mind the following:

1 The best information from evaluation can be used tomorrow or next week, so it is necessary to design the procedure to give that kind of information (though I know that sometimes the lessons may only dawn slowly).
2 Evaluation should arise if possible out of activities that are already in place. There is no excess of time to erect a whole new superstructure – goodness knows the national curriculum is going to take enough time out of the central act of teaching – but there are ways of recycling information already collected, whether in children's writing or during discussion in the classroom, for example.
3 The central evaluation is that of the curriculum. This means that we have to know what it feels like to be under the mushroom as the fertilizer showers down.
4 The department needs only the kind and the amount of information that it can handle. It can become an enormously time-consuming job to analyse questionnaires, for example, and there is a lot of pain on offer if the wrong question is asked lightly. The whole experience of evaluation should not be designed to depress. It should foster a sense of corporate worth. Shrinkage does not make us any better at our jobs.

A cooperative department

Times are much more difficult for heads of English than they were. Main professional grade and '1,265 hours' have spelt the doom of many a cooperative hope. Many main grade teachers are now very wary of taking on work that they see others being paid for, in the absence of recognition from the community at large for what they are doing. Nevertheless, a curriculum that is left to chance is likely to be fragmented, full of idiosyncrasy and personal enthusiasm but lacking coherence and pattern. Children learn to accept the strange insistence of the new teacher that things are going to be done differently from now on. They acquiesce in the expectation that they accept the mystery at the centre of the curriculum – what indeed is the meaning of it all other than the personal oddities of teachers? Some would argue that this mystification is the most appropriate training for adult life. It is, of course, a training in accepting the inadequate, in putting up with the contradictory, in settling for second best.

Where a department has joined together to make a consistent, agreed pattern of courses, it is probable that:

1 Each teacher will build on the work of the previous one with greater knowledge and confidence.
2 Each teacher will be able to defend and explain what is offered, to parents, governors, senior staff, etc.
3 The children can be taken into the secret and thus have access to its meaning. I take it that meaning is crucial to learning.
4 The courses on offer can be reviewed rationally because they are explicit rather than subliminal and private.
5 The courses are on average better than individual ones. The department can certainly capitalize on individual quality and spread its benefits.
6 There is more effective use of resources.
7 There is a positive sense of achievement among the teachers and a sense of belonging to a worthwhile enterprise.

It should be no surprise that research has repeatedly shown a positive connection between consistency and continuity of approach and the achievements of the recipients. Energy can be applied to more important deconstructions than adapting and readapting to individual teacher variation. Nor is there any reality in the belief that collaboration destroys all individuality. Rather the opposite: it liberates the individual teacher to set a personal stamp where it matters, not in the purely idiosyncratic.

Why are we here?

Even though '1,265 hours' now makes meetings matters of delicacy, there are still too many that happen because they seemed like a good idea at the time, like warm milk, but do not have either a structure or a precise purpose. Such meetings give the species a bad name and trespass on goodwill. Teachers deserve the lift that good, well run meetings can give. They can become the source of energy and a sense of purpose. They can be the single most important instrument by which the department is held together. On the other hand they can also be the visible manifestation of a department wandering in the desert, looking for who knows what.

It may help to offer some thoughts on the characteristics of meetings that add to the well-being of the department. They should:

1 Not usually be about admin matters. They can usually be put on paper or put into occasional special meetings.

2 Start from felt need. This may mean some groundwork has to be done over coffee.

3 Work from agreed documentation, where possible, such as a piece of children's writing, a set of exercise books, copies of a novel used with the second year, etc. This is particularly important where evaluation is on the agenda.

4 Keep to the agreed agenda and deadline unless there is clear agreement to change. Even then, it should be done reluctantly. Running over always creates unproductive resentment.

5 Have a moving chair so that each person in the department knows what it is like to work for agreement, to make room for everyone to speak, to forestall distraction, to keep to important matters. This also breeds a broader sense of ownership of any decisions made.

6 Conclude with resolutions and clear decisions for action. Have these written down. The last ten minutes should focus on what will be done as a result of the meeting.

7 Fix dates by which action will be taken and by whom, and what review will be taken of that action. Too often decisions wander off into the desert of good intent, to become timeless rumours. One of the essential roles of the meeting is to hold together development and review in a way that makes sense for everyone.

8 Be written up in a way that helps by being economical and cumulative. This job should also be shared around so that the sense of problem and the ownership of decisions can be shared.

9 Repeatedly remind the department of achievements.

Meetings which follow this pattern will more likely serve a living function. They are more likely to boost the sense of worthwhileness in the department as a whole and so will sustain through searching evaluations. They will be robust enough to be a major channel for the self-evaluating department.

Evaluating roles and tasks

Every teacher in an English department has a right to some feedback on his or her work. Teaching is a very isolated existence and in the nature of things there is so much to occupy the attention in the act of teaching that it is easy to lose a sense of perspective. Teachers need to be helped to see their work in context. I include the head of department in this. One way of being encouraged to stand back and review events is by setting up a series of structured conversations, at least annually. This is helped greatly if there is an accepted outline of the roles and duties of each teacher, one which has been negotiated, is public and has been reviewed from time to time. An essential feature of these conversations would be that the teacher is invited to give an evaluation first. They should not be seen as oneway delivery of judgement but as an attempt to arrive at common judgement after a consideration of the evidence. Expectation of such a periodic review should be seen as a positive chance to consider the whole direction and quality of one's work. As such there will be a powerful encouragement to prior thought, to identification of major issues, to a seeking for material that can serve as the focus for the enquiry. A review should include in its agenda the future needs of the teacher in professional development and other kinds of support.

The meeting could be prepared by the exchange of questions that each participant would like to see addressed. These questions should relate to the focus of the evaluation. Some suggestions might be:

1 What did you find the most satisfying work this year?
2 What aspects of your work do you worry about?
3 What help are you getting from myself and others?
4 Where do you see your future?
5 What do you see yourself developing next?

From the point of view of the teacher, the questions might be:

1 What is expected of me?
2 What are the criteria being employed by management to judge my work?
3 How am I doing?
4 Where am I going?
5 What can I do to improve?

For this process to be successful there would need to be a sharing, and if possible agreement, on the criteria that both will from thereon employ in the continuing evaluation of the teacher's work. As well as being well prepared, the meeting should be conducted in ways that build trust and lay the foundations for further action by both parties. Notes should be kept of the conversation, but these should be shared and open to challenge. Indeed, challenge should be a part of the conversation, for every teacher has a right to more than just cosy reinforcement. If the support is handled well there will be natural opportunities to challenge as well.

A well run evaluation interview will have the following characteristics:

1 It will be negotiable.
2 It will have a shared agenda.
3 There will be the intention to review at a later date.
4 There will be room for both support and challenge.
5 It will agree a set of actions to be taken by each participant.

The object of these reviews is not to arrive at a devastatingly honest appraisal; but they should seek to increase the amount of shared knowledge. The aim is to identify progress and find achievable ambitions. Evaluation is an educative process and we should bear in mind that we all face up to difficulties better when we have confidence that we are in general making progress.

The evaluation of resource decisions

Every decision taken about resources has consequences in what cannot be bought and in the time it takes out of teachers. There is no decision that does not have costs and penalties. How are decisions made between alternatives? How are the consequences of the decision recorded and analysed? It can be a delegated task to do just that.

For instance, what are the costs of buying a set of coursebooks? There are obviously other resources that can no longer be afforded, but how much of each of the new books is ever employed? How many of the department actually use them and how often? There needs to be a rather more rigorous enquiry than the matter usually gets.

What are the consequences of a particular book-issuing system? If a system is a loose one in order to ease access and flexibility, how does that affect losses? If the system is more rigid, how much more time is spent by teachers? Is a consequence that less time is spent using books than is felt acceptable? These are matters not just of finance, though that is important. They also concern the best use of scarce teacher time. They concern the balance of time and curricular intentions. Every curriculum decision has time costs. In some cases these are unacceptable when set against what is delivered.

Even such a trivial matter as the kind of paper that is to be used, whether file paper or exercise books, which may seem to be without penalty, turns out to be complex when looked at properly.

Evaluation in these areas can often have hard consequences in the battle for resources in the school as a whole. A department that has done its homework about real costs and consequences is more likely to be able to present a hard headed claim for serious consideration. However, it is not only intra-departmental information that is required. The head of department will also want to know how much other departments are allowed, by what formula monies are allocated, how that compares with other English departments in other schools. When local financial management puts so many of these decisions in the hands of governors, there will be an even greater need to know.

Involving the learner

Where possible the information already available in the school can be used incidentally to provide information which helps in the evaluation of the depart-ment. It is normal good practice that every child is asked to exercise some self-assessment as part of the English course. This is no longer seen as a frill, now that we know that the learner who reflects on learning will be a more powerful learner. The additional value is that such a process will inevitably provide insights into how the curriculum is received. So will any sensitively compiled profile. The better the design of the profile (including pupil contributions) the more certain will be the fall out of evaluative information.

There are other ways of involving the learners. For instance, ask a number of children to keep a record of the occasions upon which they are asked to talk in various ways. The emergent picture can be used for across-department comparisons. It will throw up all sorts of questions as to the value, the nature, the variety of talk. Another real language task is to ask a number to write their initial thoughts when faced with a writing task. This is not to say that whatever is said is the whole truth about how writing can be perceived; but it will certainly be part of the truth and should not be suppressed or ignored. Both of these are real activities, concerned with language for real purposes, as is asking pupils to write a specification on how their writing could be most helpfully marked. If the teacher then follows the specification, the next question would be, 'What have you learnt from this? Have you changed your mind?' This is a real task, worth inclusion in the curriculum in its own right, yet throwing light on the received curriculum. There are many ways in which the curriculum will be enriched by asking learners to reflect. Even more powerfully, if courses are visibly changed as a result of helpful comment, this will reinforce children's view that their words have effects. Can there be a more crucial language lesson?

In conclusion

A department that moves in an energetic way into the evaluation of its work will be the stronger for it. I do not see why we should be so secretive about what we do and the way that we do it. Everyone benefits by increased clarity of mind and stronger foundations. English teachers have not been good advocates, paradoxically, for English teachers are among the most eloquent. Evidence, not rhetoric, is the way to persuasion. Good work will be the stronger for scrutiny and bad work will be seen for what it is. There really is no need to hang on to the inferior just because we have fought battles on its behalf. If a particular approach falls under the weight of evidence, out it should go. The time can be used better in more fertile activities. Where the evidence supports our strongly defended methods, they will emerge all the stronger for it.

Notes

1 M. Donaldson (1978) *Children's Minds*, London: Fontana.
2 E. Lunzer and K. Gardner (1979) *The Effective Use of Reading*, London: Heinemann Educational for the Schools Council.

PART TWO
Oracy

2 Perspectives on oracy

ALAN HOWE

I have entitled this piece 'Perspectives on oracy' because what I want to try and do is to look at children's talk in school from a number of different perspectives and to raise a number of issues connected with those perspectives.

I'd like to start by telling a story, a version of which I first heard told by Mike Newby. It's called *Raucous Little Sister*.

I'd like you to imagine a large Victorian house in the centre of Cheltenham: three storeys and a basement. There is a family living in this house; the father has married twice – two daughters by his first marriage and a younger daughter by his second marriage. Unfortunately the second wife died, the father's away on business a lot and the two elder sisters are the ones who rule the roost, forcing their younger sister to do all of the menial, dirty tasks around the house. It's the two elder sisters who go out into society and get invited to things and the younger sister who is always left at home. She's called 'raucous little sister' because she's always chattering, singing to herself little rhymes, little songs, talking to the neighbours over the fence and so on – but she never gets invited anywhere. Let's call her two elder sisters 'Ms Reading' and 'Ms Writing', and of course you know what happens: in 1985 all three of them get invited to the GCSE ball. The invites drop through the letter box and the little sister opens hers frantically and she says 'I've been invited to the Ball; finally, finally I've been recognized!'

'Oh, it's ridiculous, it must be a computer error', say her two elder sisters.

She says, 'No, it's true, Sir Keith says come along to the GCSE ball.'

'Well anyway', they say, 'you can't come – you have nothing to wear', and you of course know what happens: they go off to the GCSE ball and the younger sister is left distraught.

But along comes a fairy godmother and suddenly she is transformed and has new clothes to wear.

She arrives at the GCSE ball late and it's in full swing. She enters through the double doors, walks across the hall and the prince (or shall we say Kingman?) sees her. He thinks, 'Who is she? I haven't seen her before, she's beautiful, I must get to know her.' He walks across to her and looks her in the eyes and says, 'I don't know who you are. You're beautiful, you must dance with me.'

She looks at him quizzically, then eventually answers, 'Yes, I will dance with you but don't forget you have got to assess me as well.'

'Fine, I'm prepared to assess you', the prince replies, 'but don't forget that you have got to satisfy my criteria.'

In a sense that is what has happened to talk. Talk has been the Cinderella of the language modes for years and years. It is commonplace in school, we have all recognized it, we have even recognized its usefulness but when it comes to going out in society, when it comes to being invited to the ball, talk has been left behind. In the last four years or so, GCSE oral communication, the importance placed on active learning approaches through such initiatives as TVEI, and, more recently, the establishment of a national oracy project, with over thirty LEAs developing their own locally based initiatives, have all contributed to a situation in which the spoken word is being given much greater prominence in educational thinking and planning.

In addition, a number of official publications have recently provided us with a number of positive statements about the importance of the spoken word in education. We can read this in the recently produced draft guidelines for English 5–11 in the national curriculum: 'Interactive spoken language is widely recognized as a powerful means of learning. It also, obviously, is essential in the world outside school.'[1]

In the *Guidelines for Science 5–16* produced by the National Curriculum Working Party for Science the following assertions are made:

Children's scientific ideas do not develop only through first-hand experiences. Communication with others plays an important part in the learning process. Children's learning is supported through discussion with peers and adults. Through talk and informal writing they are able to make their ideas clearer to themselves, as well as making them available for reflection, discussion, and checking.'[2]

So where are we now? We are at a stage where spoken language in school has got some kind of official sanctioning – it's been officially legitimized. Cinderella has been invited to the ball. Why is that? Why suddenly would spoken language have this official recognition? I would like to think that it is because it is now generally recognized that children need to articulate their ideas, to make them their own; because it is recognized that children need to have their own vernacular language valued in the classroom; because it is generally recognized that children need to be given power over language, so that they can learn to discuss, to argue, to negotiate, to persuade, to respond in discussion, to resist and challenge spurious arguments, learn to ask questions, learn to engage critically with the world. I would like to think it is to do with all those things, but I somehow doubt it; and as well as this upsurge of activity and of initiatives and the very positive statements we get in official documents, we also get mixed messages, contradictory statements. For example, have a look at this extract from the Kingman Report:

36. In a class of 11-year-olds visited by the Committee, the pupils had been divided into groups of four to discuss whether the rights of individuals are threatened by establishing No Smoking areas in public places. One member of each group was elected to provide a summary of that group's discussion. The elected reporter gave a one-minute summary of his or her group's discussion, standing up in front of the class (with the lights at the front of the class being dipped 10 seconds before the minute was up). Each summary was then commented on by a member of another group, in terms of, for example:

- how clear the summary was
- whether the speaker kept repeating the same structure or vocabulary
- whether the speaker made the discussion appear interesting
- whether the speaker represented only one point of view or was able to represent several points of view
- whether the speaker stood up straight and looked at all members of the audience or kept looking just to one side of the class
- whether the speaker was fluent or paused too much
- whether the speaker was adequately audible at the back
- whether the speed of the speech was appropriate

After each critique, other members of the class offered their observations, often including a critique of 'unjust' criticisms made by the previous speaker. This was clearly a familiar format and most pupils participated.[3]

It is as if children come to school with a language that is a bit like cholera. The job of teachers and schools is to engage in some kind of inoculation programme – to root out the debased forms. There is a view in this extract that suggests that there is a particular kind of spoken language that is better than another and the job of teachers is to replace the kind of language children come to school with, with this more acceptable form. There's also a focus on surface features and even some elements of an 'elocution model' of the spoken language. In a recent letter in the *Times Educational Supplement* the writer complained about the 'slovenliness of speech' exhibited by some school leavers heard on the radio, and offered the following solution:

Schools are their only hope. It would not take much time, though it would need persistence. A few speech exercises run through as a matter of course at the beginning of every English lesson, for instance, will soon train pupils in proper attention to consonants.

In a book entitled *Teaching Talk*, Gillian Brown *et al.* propose a hierarchical approach to the 'teaching' of the spoken language:

Since most pupils perform inadequately in transferring information in at least some types of information-related speech, we believe they should be explicitly taught to control the transfer of information in information-related speech.

If they are to be taught, then a syllabus must be devised. It is clear that the syllabus should be structured, so that pupils learn first to perform relatively simple acts of information transfer, and only gradually move towards the extremely demanding types of task . . . The main aim of this book is to discuss how such a graded syllabus can be devised.[4]

I would like to contrast this perspective with a very different perspective offered by Douglas Barnes:

> It is when the pupil is required to use language to grapple with new experience or to order old experience in a new way that he is most likely to find it necessary to use language differently. And this will be very different from taking over someone else's language in external imitation of its forms: on the contrary, it is the first step towards new patterns of thinking and feeling, new ways of representing reality to himself . . .[5]

Here the emphasis is on using language for real purposes as part of the learning process, and the suggestion is that two things might happen: by using language in this way children are likely to learn more effectively and are also, simultaneously as it were, likely to develop as talkers and listeners – to develop their language use.

Now in a sense that has been the starting point of the work that we have been doing in the Wiltshire oracy project. We have tried to say to ourselves 'What does that mean in practice in the classroom, and how can we translate the implications of that into classroom practice?'

I want to take a slight sideways shift at this point, and just briefly say something about the word 'oracy' itself. In considering what we might mean by 'development' it might be useful to have some kind of map of the territory. The following is an attempt to devise some kind of 'oracy map'. Like all maps it is an oversimplified version of reality.

The four dimensions are actually interlocking. The first is what I have called 'learning' – this is the connection between the spoken language and understanding. Very often talking through something can help to clarify it – or even generate new ways of thinking about it. We can use talk to formulate ideas, to grasp at semiperceived thoughts and bring them into existence. One way of viewing talk in school is as a necessary bridge between the experiences and values that the pupil brings into the classroom and the experiences, concepts, understanding being met for the first time in school.

The second dimension is 'resources', 'the linguistic nuts and bolts' of oracy – the ability to use appropriate vocabulary; to use the spoken language for a variety of purposes; the ability to use non-verbal signs – gestures, eye contact and so on; the ability to 'organize' ideas in talk; the ability to switch register and code according to context.

'Reciprocity' is a clumsy word but the best that I have come across to describe this third dimension which is the 'interpersonal or social' side of oracy – working with others, getting on with other people, being a good listener as well as a good talker. You could say that oracy is as much about facilitating the word of others as it is about talking yourself. It is about helping other people say what they want to say in all sorts of ways.

The fourth dimension is 'reflexivity'. There are two sides to this. Firstly, 'being reflective', using the spoken language to be reflective about your learning, doing

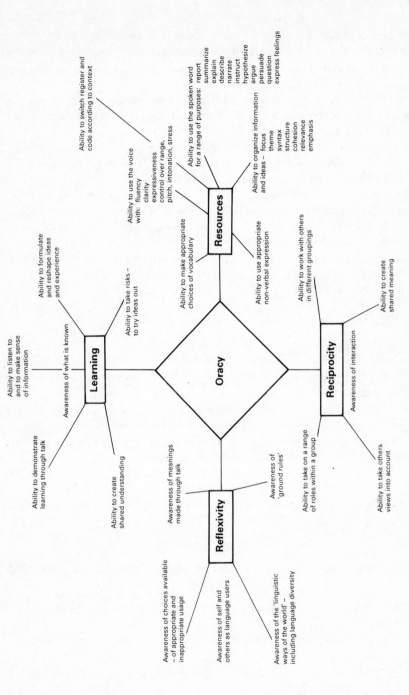

Figure 2.1   An oracy map

what Jerome Bruner has described as 'looking back on your traces and telling yourselves what you know' through talk. This is an often neglected aspect of function of talk in the classroom, but one which has very powerful possibilities. So – being reflective *through* talk – but also linked with this is the ability to be reflective about yourself and others as talkers and listeners: to be *aware* of yourself and to be aware of *others* as talkers and listeners. It does seem to me that this is one of the key ingredients in developing children's oracy.

It may be that this map might be a useful starting point when we are beginning to think about where children's language might be developing, and how we as teachers might be able to assist in this process.

You can sum all of this up in one word – versatility. If you take this map of oracy and ask, 'what in the end might we be hoping to move children towards?', I would argue that we should be helping to move them towards being more versatile users of the spoken language, being able to make their language meet the demands of a wide variety of situations. So when I talk about versatility it is that sort of ability that I mean – the ability to make your language meet the demands of both the known and the unfamiliar.

What can we learn from early language development?

Before we start devising grandiose plans for achieving that, before we start devising graded syllabuses and slotting in oracy as another bit of the curriculum jigsaw, I think it is useful to remind ourselves of what happens in the first four or five years of a child's life, before she actually arrives at school. Most children come to school already very effective talkers and listeners in the contexts in which they have grown up and the situations they have had to use talk for. If five-year-olds coming into the school have managed to master most of the grammar of the language, have an active vocabulary of about three to five thousand words, have understood many of the nuances and the subtleties of the language without any formal teaching, it might be useful to ask ourselves what has contributed to that and what we as teachers in schools can learn from it.

In a chapter of his book *Fair Dinkum Teaching and Learning*, entitled 'Oracy in Australian schools', Garth Boomer provides us with a list of 'The conditions most likely . . .' – features of the language climate in the early years which seem to be particularly conducive to language development.[6] The list includes the following:

1 'Tracking', where the adults try to work out what the child is seeking to say, or talk themselves as a commentary to accompany the child's activity.
2 'Caring and sharing' – which follows on from the previous condition, the adults engaging in activities along with the child.
3 'Talk serving needs' – obviously one of the reasons children learn to talk so effectively is that they very quickly realize that they can alter their world as a result of particular utterances. When my two-year-old daughter says 'potty', it must seem to her as if she's uttered a magical phrase, so quickly do her parents start to attend to her!

4 'Adult time' – it seems to me that it is not so much the amount of time that is important as time spent with caring adults who are doing all of the above things as well as modifying their language, and their usual ways of responding to language, in order to give the language learner the opportunity to make meaning. Even parents of new-born babies start to behave with them as if the infant was an ideal conversational partner! Is it not strange that adult members of the species have long conversations with tiny members of the same species who do not speak the language? Of course, what we are doing is treating the child as an ideal conversational partner because we know intuitively that this is the best way of helping the child to learn all the complex skills involved in spoken interaction.

5 'Words to play with': children are quick to see language as a kind of playdough, a medium you can mess about with. This is partly because they get pleasure from rolling the sounds around, but I suspect it is more serious than that. In breaking the rules the child is learning them, and is attending to communication itself – it is a kind of code cracking.

6 'Challenge and involvement' – Children need a stake in what they say, to be using the language for real purposes.

7 'A wide range of contexts' – to put it simply, language will grow in proportion to the breadth and depth of experiences the child is having, and the opportunity she is given to talk about a range of topics and to engage with others who are using talk for a variety of purposes.

8 'Exploratory talk' – asking questions and getting serious answers, using talk to hypothesize, to speculate about things, to take risks.

What seems to be emerging from this analysis, then, is the crucial importance, in early language learning, of mature speakers engaging seriously with the child and providing her with various kinds of verbal scaffolding within which she can try her language out for size. The adult role is one of being 'reciprocal' – following the child as she talks and providing her with what Gordon Wells has called 'sustaining strategies' as a way of helping the speaker do her own extending.

In what ways might these insights inform our teaching?

And so to school

When we get to school, of course, we find that the picture is not quite as rosy as it might be.

HMI have this to say:

> The National Secondary Survey recorded curricula in many schools which, especially in years 4 and 5 [now referred to as 10 and 11], were heavily dominated by writing, largely of a kind requiring notes and summaries. In consequence, talk tended to be squeezed out, especially that type of talk which helps young people to handle new ideas, to develop a reasoned argument, to internalize their experiences and to find personal expression for them.[7]

Unfortunately, it does seem that when you look at the school system as children move up through it talk does get squeezed out of the classroom. There are, of course, lots of reason why this happens.

Why is talk not encouraged? When I have asked this question of groups of teachers, these are the sorts of answers they give:

1 Concerns about noise, lack of control or handing over control, discipline problems and so on.
2 Syllabus constraints and lack of time, particularly in the secondary school.
3 The exam system: when it comes down to it in the secondary school particularly you show what you know you can do by picking up a pen and writing.
4 The difficulty of evaluating what is happening.
5 Organizational difficulties to do with space, layout of chairs and so on.
6 The fact that talk has got a life of its own; you cannot guarantee what pupils will do. This is a concern to do with control over knowledge and over what counts as being relevant in the classroom.
7 Finally, entrenched attitudes to methodology. In other words, teachers who operate with a model of learning which does not admit that talk is a vital part of the learning process. If you do not have that it seems to me that all of these other constraints are likely to get in the way. On the other hand, if you do have a view of the learning process which admits the importance of talk, that immediately enables you to start overcoming some of these other barriers – they are not insurmountable.

Some of these objections are obviously deeply rooted as part of the system we work in. Some of them are things you can overcome in your own classroom. More important than all of that is the need to recognize that all teachers everywhere suffer from these sorts of constraints and that there is no point in feeling guilty about it. Once you actually get over that business of feeling guilty then very often you can begin to find ways round some of the problems that are presented by talk.

Getting the climate right for talk

Most of the research evidence points to the fact that pupils are rarely given opportunities to engage with a variety of spoken language contexts as part of their regular school experiences. What this reminds us of is the fact that the curriculum and the way it is taught are pretty impervious to change. To extend the metaphor a little, we can see the curriculum as a kind of solid bedrock covered by the soil of learning – rich and fertile in parts, but also with large areas of thin, poorly cultivated soil. Talk is one of the essential nutrients – without it there is little long-term growth and only the strongest plants manage to prosper. In such a situation, what is needed is not a bulk order for more watering cans, but a change in climate!

What is involved in achieving this – or at least in beginning to take the first steps? Having worked with a number of groups of teachers who have been tackling the challenge, I would like to offer a few tentative thoughts in response to this question myself.

1 Learning first, talk second – it is what talk can do for our pupils, as well as what they can do with talk, that is our main concern. Oracy is important, but not as important as understanding. The two kinds of development – learning through, and learning to use, are intertwined.

2 Excitement and development of talk first, assessment second. We need to ask 'what kinds of talk (and writing, reading, thinking) do I want to stimulate in my classroom', and then 'How can I assess these?'

3 A repertoire of teaching approaches – we need to be on the alert for talking and listening opportunities as part of a wider repertoire of teaching and learning strategies. Oracy should be seen not as instead of other activities, but as one of a number of ways of helping pupils to make and communicate meaning. We also need to be aware of the particular value of talk as a way of exploring and sharing understanding – what we might call 'shared drafting' – and of reshaping and presenting understanding with others. There will be times when it is more appropriate for pupils to be silently reading, writing, listening to the teacher, and others when they will be busily talking, often within the same lesson or activity.

4 Flexible classrooms – in order to ensure that talk can be one of a number of currents of activity, classrooms will need to be flexible enough to allow for individual, pair, small-group and whole-class activities. Teachers will need to be flexible enough both to plan for such activities and to adapt what they are doing when the occasion arises. (One science colleague of mine said recently that the major shift of perspective he had undergone as a result of being involved in the Wiltshire oracy project was that 'now when I run out of things for the class to do I think of something they can talk about'). In addition we need to build in flexible, open ended sequences of work which lend themselves both to classroom-based and out of school contexts for talk.

5 The task's the thing – we need to recognize the importance of context, and the way the spoken word is influenced by the nature of the task and the behaviour of the other participants (including ourselves). Because talk is usually inter-active, we have far less control as speakers over what we say than we do in writing – we can be interrupted, sidetracked, steamrollered, ignored or we can receive offputting non-verbal signals which make us lose confidence, or lose our drift. It is consequently important that we try to set up conditions which are likely to work in favour of pupils' talk rather than against it. This certainly involves being able to seize the chance to build in some talk when the occasion arises, but it also means that we need to plan carefully for providing a range of opportunities. Oracy will not feature centrally if we leave it solely to chance or if we provide the pupils with vague, unfocused instructions, purposes and outcomes. If we want to encourage pupils to learn how to develop a reasoned argument, or to establish a hypothesis, then we need to think carefully about

setting up tasks and contexts which are most likely to elicit this kind of talk.

6   Teacher intervention – we need to know when to intervene, when to keep out – and how. As a rough rule of thumb I tend to intervene less at the initial stages, reserving my interventions to the sorting out of groups which are having trouble getting started, and get more involved when pupils are ready to try their ideas out. The way in which we intervene can be crucial too. Individuals or groups of pupils will respond very differently to being asked 'How are you getting on? Any problems?' (Teacher in stereotypical role as trouble shooter and assessor), compared to 'Tell me about what you've found out?' (Teacher as listener – what I've called the 'attentive passenger'[8] role, in which the pupils are encouraged to take the driving seat, and the teacher adopts the stance of an intelligent, interested and at times knowledgeable listener.) Pupils can so often feel powerless in interaction with an adult, particularly a teacher who 'knows it all already'. It can require a great effort on our part to counter the many ways in which schools make pupils feel that they don't have a legitimate voice in the learning process.

There are no hard and fast rules for this, of course – different teachers will develop their own styles for intervening and joining in as part of pupil talk. To illustrate this, here are some comments by a science teacher, reflecting on his role in promoting learning through talk in his lessons:

> If you want discussion to fail in your classroom, keep a low profile, put vague or ambiguous questions to the whole group, and take responses only from the chosen few. The most successful sessions I have experienced have seen me maintaining a high profile, wandering through the groups, clearly 'listening in' and occasionally joining in, pushing where necessary, chiding where the occasion demands, encouraging. No one in the class dares to believe they are not observed and are likely to be called upon. This is not as threatening as it sounds. It is just that if I value the activity then I will be vigorous in encouraging involvement. It is, after all, part of my role as a teacher.[9]

What this all adds up to, then, is that if we want to encourage our pupils to talk, we have got to behave differently. Oracy will have more chance of flourishing in the classroom if we can succeed in providing a richer variety of roles for both sets of participants in the teaching and learning interaction.

Some suggestions for pupil roles:

1   Pupils working to their own agenda – having a personal stake in the activity, being provided with some degree of choice over what they are doing and how they are going to tackle it.

2   Pupils as experts – talking about what they know to someone who does not know. As well as the exploratory talk mentioned earlier, we need also to build in opportunities for more sustained talk, when there's a 'press' on the pupils' language, a demand, recognized by the pupils, that what is said needs to take

into account the state of knowledge of the listeners and thus requires a degree of explicitness not necessary in collaborative talk.

3 Pupils 'in role' – through the use of drama approaches, simulations. This can have the effect of helping them to say things they would never otherwise have said, in fresh ways.

The radical shift

Although a commitment to oracy *is* about techniques and strategies that we might try to build in, it is also much more than this. If we are serious about committing ourselves to children's spoken language, bringing it into the centre of education, allowing the child's voice to have more of a part to play, that entails a radical shift in our expectations of children, in the way we go about organizing learning in our classrooms and the sorts of roles that are taken on by both teachers and pupils.

That is a major challenge. I think the important thing is for the teacher to begin to make the first steps and to recognize that there are ways of actually moving in that direction without feeling that it is too oppressive an idea.

We are at a most interesting time in the field of language and education, with the real possibility of the right sorts of developments being encouraged on the ground in schools which might begin to lead to 'the radical shift'. As will have become clear from what I have written so far, this is an issue that transcends the concerns of English departments in the secondary school, and is the rightful concern of all teachers. As another of the teachers who has been involved in the Wiltshire oracy project has written: 'We need to make oral approaches part of the stock in trade of all teachers, and in so doing help to make pupils more active in their learning.'[10]

I started this piece by calling it 'Perspectives on oracy'. I have no doubt that the perspective that has developed gradually among those of us who have been working in Wiltshire has begun to seep through what I have been writing. In the end, of course, the story has only just begun. Maybe the tide is shifting for oracy in new and vigorous ways. There are, however, equally powerful voices which would pull us in a different direction. Cinderella has been invited to the ball – the question is, which tune is she going to be asked to dance to?

1 Loose talk: towards implementing and managing a policy for oracy
KEN WILBY

Our school is a mixed community comprehensive of 1,200. English is taught in mixed ability classes throughout. Recently, despite a long association with oral work, the department I head began to share a growing dissatisfaction with current practice. Superficially, the impetus for change arose from the demands of the separately accredited oral component of the GCSE, but its roots went far deeper. Oracy seemed to be largely uncharted territory. There were some useful signposts from NATE through meetings and publications but it was the work of the Wiltshire oracy project that offered the first clear, if confessedly incomplete, maps. We warmed to several aspects of the project's work: the insistence on regarding oracy as something far more fundamental to the learning process than merely another subject; the close and continuous involvement of teachers working within their own schools; and the conscious blend of theory and practice. In the wake of GCSE, there was considerable disquiet about the 'cascade' model of training; the Wiltshire project offered an alternative.

In our English department we decided against a grand plan; we had neither the time, the experience nor the inclination to be systematic. We wanted to explore, and so to try to establish some working principles about the best conditions for releasing talk, class management and effective teacher intervention. Accordingly we pursued interests, followed hunches and drew on experience, sometimes as individuals, sometimes collectively. Many seeds were planted and while some took root, others did not. Distinct areas of interest emerged: narratology, as defined by Harold Rosen in *Stories and Meanings*[11], which centred on 'story circles'; self-evaluation and self-assessment; pupil perception of talk; the teaching of literature; and finally, the relationship between process and product or performance.

Although most of the work we undertook was aimed at developing practical classroom ideas which we could make and use, it also came to provide, for some members of the department, a focus for part-time academic study, a dimension we had not anticipated but one which was to prove mutually enriching. There is insufficient space here to recount our work in detail, only enough to draw on a few examples, signal some of the issues and reflect on tentative conclusions.

The first concerns resourcing. We quickly became aware that in order to pursue our aims we had to overcome some serious classroom management problems: we were hopelessly lacking in hardware. We had an assortment of odds and ends and some high quality equipment available from the school's central AVA store, but several of our ideas necessitated taping pupil talk, small group work and routine access. So we decided to buy enough cassette-recorders, distribution units and headphones to allow us to create, in minutes, a portable and flexible language lab. It proved to be a good move but, at the time, out of the normal annual department budget, it seemed done at the expense of an awful lot of books.

'Tooling up' in this way changed what we could do and how we could do it. Pupils could now make, unmake and listen to their own tapes as well as using prerecorded material as and when appropriate, either as a class, in groups or as individuals. Crucially, it allowed control of pacing, editing, reviewing and evaluating to move into the hands of the users. Practically, it allowed us to begin to encourage our pupils to reflect on their own use of spoken language and to extend that range of use. We developed the idea of a kind of talking language log to promote greater understanding of that most important of all dialogues, that within ourselves.

We got pupils used to the idea of recording their own discussions in class. It was important that these discussions rose naturally out of on-going work, rather than as set pieces. So it might be group talk about *Romeo and Juliet*, role-play, response to video and so on. The recorded discussions were then used to locate the starting point for the next session. We gave time to review and reflect upon what had been said previously. Once initial awkwardnesses were overcome these talk logs came to be seen as both useful and interesting to the pupils. They began quite naturally to comment on the way things had gone, to talk about talk.

We developed this process by making the group work as genuinely collaborative as possible, so that the progress of the individual was dependent upon the working of the group. In this way, we upped the stakes. This put a pressure on collective decision making, problem solving and sharing of ideas within the group and also encouraged the pupils to review their own talk. They began to evaluate, criticize and explore group dynamics. They began to see, too, when making a taped record was preferable to written records, which in turn led to profitable discussion about the differences and similarities between written and spoken language. Most important of all, it got the youngsters thinking and talking about themselves as language users, the way that language has power, that it can include but also exclude others. Here, talk was part of the very fabric of the learning and because it was contextualized it was meaningful.

We began to look at the way we taught literature with this in mind. We were interested in structuring group work more rigorously, widening the range of contexts for talk and tapping the potential for learning. We experimented with some of the ideas in 'jigsaw', and wrote lessons on a range of poetry as different as Shakespeare, Hardy and Spender. The idea of the 'home' and 'expert' flexible grouping was new to us. Because of the common focus and individual accountability that Slavin[12] insists on the talk was collaborative and contextualized. It also led to high quality written work of a very diverse nature.

The pupils knew in advance that there would be a number of outcomes: an oral assessment drawn from the group work; a personal response to the poem; and finally some self-evaluative work. Marina, a very perceptive pupil, wrote a very impressive critical response to 'The Darkling Thrush', earning praise from the teacher, which made her discomfort with her subsequent oral assessment all the more confusing to her. Her essay was full of ideas which were conspicuously absent from the writing of the other members of her home group, for which she was penalized in discussion with the teacher: she had failed to meet the criterion of sharing. A point was being made, of course, and Marina was first mature enough to see it, then intrigued. Like the others, she then wrote an analytical piece about the group work, her relationships and her thoughts during the lesson, which was a genuine reflection on learning and which her teacher considered to be a very significant moment for her.

If pupils perceive that talk is important to us, that it has status, they will respond; but if they suspect it to be irrelevant to the main business, many will hold back if only becase talk of the kind we want to generate is hard work. For talk to prosper, we must take an active role, first in developing schemes of work which facilitate talk and second in controlling the environment for talk. This means providing the security without which few pupils will risk making themselves vulnerable. Here is Penny, a fourth-year girl of average academic ability reflecting on her own development as part of her self evaluation:

> I am now able to listen and talk with more understanding and find this is one of my strong points in the subject. For one of the first times in my life I am able to talk and people listen to what I say and seriously consider what I have said. This has given me confidence.

We have to work hard at creating a sympathetic environment for talk. We have to intervene so that we create the conditions in which pupils will take risks and embrace speculative utterances, exploration and uncertainty. Oracy does not develop evenly and steadily or as a result of regular measured practice, rather as one learns to play a musical instrument. Instead oracy develops in bursts or explosively and what is needed is a 'press' on language which forces new modes of expression and pushes back boundaries. Penny's sense of success arose not from a steady flow of good oral marks but from having experienced one or two moments of fluency and articulation which surprised and excited her and the power of which both she an her peers deeply understood. Every child should be encouraged to discover the power of the spoken word in all its forms and by so doing discover his or her own voice. This requires explicit groundrules and the right balance between freedom and constraint in the classroom.

Making demands had its difficulties, because it brought us hard up against our own attitudes and values. We needed to be persistent as well as consistent. Here is another girl called Lisa. It is clear that she falters a little – she finds it tough:

> My oral work has a lot to be desired, I am shy in oral work. Myself, I think I am good at listening but when it comes to talking I lose confidence. I need to boost my confidence a bit.

Lisa shows an awareness of the importance of talk and its relation to listening. Her comments are not resistant, hostile or defeatist but reveal the importance that she attaches to her genuine difficulties with talk.

Of course it soon became apparent that the focus on classroom talk meant teacher-talk and teaching style. If there were any doubts about the need they were quickly dispelled. Even when we were trying to let go of the conch, it seems that we continually underestimated just how much talking we did. Mandy: 'I do not talk out much in class. This is not because I do not know what to say, it is not because I am embarrassed, it is because you don't give me chance.'

As an extension of this kind of work, taped homework began to appear. Sometimes pupils worked on their own, other times they produced collaborative pieces. The obvious next step was to issue all the pupils with their own tapes for such purposes, either as supplements to homework, or, increasingly, as the homework itself. The ubiquitous plastic carrier bag could no longer cope: there was a danger of losing work and a continual struggle to fish it out of the bottom of the bag. So we bought cassette carrying cases. This meant we could store the tapes sensibly.

All this is a far cry from the stilted ten minute set piece on football hooliganism, but, of course oral work is about the product as well as process of talk. We wanted to avoid superficial posturing, to encourage not 'selling' but making. Performance has its own rigorous demands and disciplines but any drama teacher will tell you that children find their own voices and learn to understand other voices by making rather than imitating; they find commitment through emotional and intellectual investment. Performance is best this way and provides the link with genuine eloquence.

The best performance tapes we experienced arose as extensions of personal writing. Some were short stories but mainly they were poetry. The writing came first as an end in itself; only then did the pupils consider the notion of creating programmes of anthologies for the listener. The skills and requirements are daunting. They identified audience, sustained and varied mood, identified register and effective pacing, selected and integrated incidental music, utilized and wrote link narrative, they shaped and they directed. They recorded, reviewed and 'redrafted' – much as we do when we write. The results were excellent. Of course the products were more personal, more important and better than the hastily recorded set piece. If we want to catch pupils thinking on their feet to 'test' them then focus on the genuinely contextualized discussion; if we want to assess performance give real performance disciplines. Performers are their own hardest critics.

Oracy is no panacea – we knew that before we started. It is so important to try to get it right, though. A department colleague with over twenty years in the classroom, put it this way:

> Everyone tends to think about how talk can help everything else the kids do in school, and that's right in a way; in another more important way it's the wrong emphasis, what really matters for the kids, is the talk and what everything else can do for it.

2   Media education and information technology as sites for oral work
NICHOLAS ROBERTS

Are you ready?

Motherhands will whack you, motherhands will crack you . . .

Look soulfully up through your eyebrows, blow out your cheeks to resemble a

cloyingly cute four-year-old and sing the above in a Fairy Liquid voice –
preferably to the theme tune from *My Little Pony*.

Watching a group of four largish boys and two serious girls attempt this was
one of the incidental pleasure of a media project I undertook with my mixed
ability English class of thirteen-year-olds last year: our tribute to Christmas and
the mass marketing which it triggers. The English department in this 11–18
comprehensive had taken the decision to extend its traditional emphasis on work
on the mass media with fourth and fifth years to all age levels and to create a
coherent programme for dealing with aspects such as the differences between
media, ideas about audience and how the world is represented in media products.
At the same time, money was found to purchase a half share in a BBC
microcomputer and printer which could be shifted between the rooms of the
eleven teachers working in the lower school building.

2T had had an unsettled first year of English in the school, with a split
timetable and change of teacher, so we spent the first half of the autumn term
working calmly on our individual choices of fiction. I wanted an activity for the
second half which would encourage group cooperation and develop a language
emphasis: after some debate within the class about their television watching
habits we decided to focus on the huge pre-Christmas advertising campaigns
aimed squarely at them and their younger brothers and sisters. As a matter of
perspective I was able to note that news of an education support grant for IT had
reached the schools; this proved, for the whole country, to be slightly less than the
amount spent on promoting Sindy dolls in the run up to the festive season.

My targets were:

1 group cohesion;
2 analytical skills in confronting media products;
3 extended capacity with language;
4 confidence in using IT.

What happened fell into three stages, successful in locking on to media issues, but
most satisfying and absorbing in provoking a range of oral activity, some of it
intense and of high quality. For the first lesson of the sequence, I invited our
media studies advisory teacher to help us investigate the constructed nature of
television adverts; a task he performed very effectively by asking us to reconstruct
one from the soundtrack alone. Within ten minutes the pupils were heavily
absorbed in talk about talk – the soundtrack included some speech – and talk
about lyrics: Cher singing 'I got you, babe' readily signalled for them the
aggressively stereotypical images of a girl lost without her boy which appeared in
the actual advert's minisaga of playground heartbreak amongst six-year-olds.

The second stage, which ran for two weeks, began with a brief demonstration
of a database programme and set groups of four pupils to plan, collect, structure
and feed into the computer a range of information on toy marketing which could
then be interrogated by the whole class (and a parallel class doing a similar project

with another teacher). Here the addition of a computer to the classroom equation shifted the oral environment considerably. I noticed:

1 The computer shifted the focus away from the teacher – talk became freer, faster and more effective. Although most of the activity took place away from the machine, the centre of gravity in the room had been relocated.
2 The computer placed a 'press' on language, lent urgency and a sense of using real tools for their work – groups had to evolve a strategy for their talk, negotiate tasks, record decisions. Talk became more important in their eyes, more deliberate, more consciously about action.
3 The word-processing programme created space for talk – between the act of creating and the act of recording. The volatility of talk, its zigzags, were matched by the ability of the programme to add, subtract, move words around.
4 The database demands precision – in entering information and in interrogation – yet it also allowed experimentation and even deliberate daftness which could be expunged. In moving group achievement onward, perhaps all talk has a legitimacy; what are the implications of this for assessment?

At the third stage, after coming together to compare findings and look at some more videotape of advertising campaigns, I invited the same groups to design for pupils slightly younger than themselves a non-gender toy, and create an outline promotional package to accompany it. I borrowed a colour printer from an art teacher who came along to show pupils how to operate it and the class's drama teacher volunteered to tailor some of her lessons with them towards the project. I also visited a couple of local toyshops for spare promotional material and back numbers of *Toy Trader*.

After the close structuring of the previous stages, I encouraged as much diversity as the children wanted: the result was an almost disappointing lull, followed by an explosion of activity with spoken language at its heart. In among the exchanges that we might expect from designing packaging, posters, logos, storyboards, etc., there were moments, indeed minutes, when the oral activity could be heard changing gear, drawn into new ratios by the demands and opportunities of the context:

Some were incidental:

1 Teachers talking to each other as one adult to another, in this case making sense of a graphics programme on the computer. Pupils joined in on a more than equal level, relinquishing the oral role of 'child' which tends to be constructed for them by teachers' public mode of speaking.

Some sprang from pupils' ideas:

2 Soundtrack talk for their own adverts, recorded by video camera, exposed the performance aspects of many speech acts, focused attention on the non-verbal. 'Didn't know all the things you did when you talked!', said Gemma, when her group added to their video their comments on what they had attempted.

Some I had hoped for:

3 Mastery of the computer itself – its language, the mysterious relationship between the visible (hardware) and the invisible (software), the things the programs could not do – all this made the users conscious of the constraints operating in other media, and drew excited and purposeful talk out of them as they collaborated on making the technology do what they wanted.

Some I had not foreseen:

4 Jingles, then lyrics, then singing became a popular activity. One group invented 'Motherhands' – an action figure with swinging arms and flat hands for punishing wayward children; it seemed only natural to move from creating the words into recording the theme tune. Something like two hours of intensive discussion and talk *about* the delivery of words went into the subsequent tape. Pupils do sing all the time of course, but only privately – it seemed that 'motherhands' had legitimized one of their favourite modes of oral expression and unlocked a real source of energy.

Case studies too readily give the impression of smoothly tailored sequences, precision timing, fluent professionalism. It was not like that at all, particularly in terms of oral activity, which had never been intended as the centre of the learning plan. Yet, in retrospect, I know that pupils had experienced this portion of their curriculum largely as and through oral events, some of it consciously so. We had set out to explore the conventions and assumptions which lay behind familiar media products, their marketing and exposure; at least some of them had not remained unspoken, or unsung.

Notes

1 DES (1988) *English for Ages 5 to 11*, London: HMSO, Section 3.17.
2 DES (1988) *Science for Ages 5 to 16*, London: HMSO, Section 2.15.
3 DES (1988) *Report of the Committee of Inquiry into the teaching of English* (The Kingman Report), London: HMSO.
4 G. Brown *et al.* (1984) *Teaching Talk – Strategies for Production and Assessment*, Cambridge: Cambridge University Press.
5 D. Barnes (1976) *From Communication to Curriculum*, London: Penguin.
6 G. Boomer (1985) *Fair Dinkum Teaching and Learning*, New Jersey: Boynton/Cook.
7 DES (1985) *The Curriculum from 5 to 16 (Curriculum Matters 2)*, London: HMSO.
8 A. Howe (1988) 'Releasing pupil talk', in *English Education*, Spring, NATE.
9 R. Essex (1987) *Oracy Matters*, Journal of the Wiltshire Oracy Project, Wiltshire LEA.
10 J. Smith (1984) *Oracy Matters*, Journal of the Wiltshire Oracy Project, Wiltshire LEA.
11 H. Rosen (1985) *Stories and Meanings*, NATE.
12 R. Slavin (1988) *School and Classroom Organisation*, Hillsdale NJ: Erlbaum.

PART THREE
Knowledge about language

3 Playing with words: a context for knowledge about language

TERRY FURLONG

As a teacher concerned with children and young people's development as language users, I have something of a confession to make about my own childhood. I have never admitted it before but ever since I first started teaching I have worried about it from time to time. And now that I am compelled to reexamine and rethink my entire world, I feel it is time to take this particular skeleton out of the cupboard and give it a good rattle. I expect that rather like gorging myself on fruit or cream buns, it never did me any good as a child – rather the reverse – but, like bunking off Sunday school, it was one of those secret pleasures I did not share with friends, let alone parents or teachers.

And the name of this secret sin? I loved doing English Language exercises. I had my own copy of *First Aid in English* with the answers in the back, and I kept the copy under my mattress so that I could do them at night with a torch under the bedclothes. And later I got secondhand copies of other similar books and enjoyed them just as much. Yet as a teacher I have always studiously avoided such books for my pupils, for what have always seemed to me very good reasons. It was not just filling in blanks, but sorting out anagrams, changing words into other words, building up families of words, guessing words from definitions, finding new words and expressions, and all the other games and puzzles I liked, even when I got them wildly wrong. In fact, getting them wrong or taking ages to do them did not matter at all because nobody else knew anyway.

In primary school when there were exercises to do, I behaved like all my friends. I groaned with boredom, got a lot wrong, had a scruffy book and terrible writing. But secretly I enjoyed them, much as I liked collecting the names of plants, flowers, birds, animals or insects and being able to identify them. But then I had lots of private interests I did not let on about to others, like poetry which I read and wrote avidly. I suppose I collected words and phrases as other little boys collected stamps or engine numbers.

Paradoxically, when it came to secondary school English lessons I did not enjoy them much at all. The books we read were pretty boring, the poems seemed lifeless, and all the rest was 'comprehension', which I hated, or parsing sentences and box analysis, which was even worse. Although I liked things like algebra, which was playing with numbers, I found no interest at all in English grammar. It was not even that I didn't understand it; I just did not see the point of it. My reaction puzzled me at the time and to a certain extent it still does. Like many teachers, English only came to life for me in the later years of school, although privately I both read and wrote quite a lot throughout my school years.

Now I am not about to equip all my long suffering pupils with copies of *First Aid in English* nor advocate a return to class exercises. I still believe strongly that people learn to listen, speak, read or write, by doing those things in a context which is real, interesting and challenging, and for purposes which they themselves consider worthwhile. What does interest me, however, is finding ways of encouraging children to step outside the language they use daily, so that they can gain another kind of power and control over it. For without this there is a risk that the language may speak them more then they speak the language.

Whenever I see pupils doing a wordsearch from a games magazine instead of the work they are supposed to be doing, or eager to make a crossword puzzle for a magazine, or writing round a word processor, or comparing how to count or how to swear in the different languages known by their friends, I am reminded of the kind of pleasure I got from playing with words. These seem to be very natural activities in which children, with differing degrees of seriousness, are playing with language and displaying something of the same fascination with it as poets and novelists do when they play with other writers' styles and devices. Like children's wicked parodies of their teachers' mannerisms and voices, it seems an essential part of trying out your equipment and seeing what you can do with it.

The difference between the English Language exercises beloved of right-wing thinktanks and the kind of playing with language which all children can enjoy seems to me to lie less in the activities themselves than in the motivations of their advocates and the contexts in which children encounter them. The attraction of exercises for tabloid leader writers is that they seem 'serious' and can be imposed on a whole class of children as a form of 'shut-'em-up-and-keep-'em-at-it' discipline. The belief that such exercises foster competition and have the incidental benefit of teaching the rules of the language, so they can write properly, helps bolster this notion of serious disciplined learning. And before too many self-satisfied grins break out, when did we last resort, in exasperation with some noisy and unruly bunch of youngsters on a Friday afternoon, to some equally boring and mindless 'comprehension' from some old book which we meant to throw out ages ago?

I will come back to comprehension later, for whether it comes in a book or whether we do it on our feet asking a class about a poem or novel they have just read, it has a lot more to do with social control in the classroom than with understanding. For the moment I want to concentrate on some of the reasons why I feel that playing with language is something all children can enjoy if the activities and circumstances are right, and why I believe that it is an essential part of gaining control and fluency in the use of language. It is too important an area of our work to abandon because of past bad practice.

One of the disappointments of the Kingman Report for me was that it spent so little time considering successful learning about language outside the school context, for that has to be the benchmark against which we measure our work as teachers inside schools. The most obvious example is the way very young children learn to speak their mother tongue, an area which has been extensively researched and thought about across a range of languages, and about the main features of which there is now a considerable measure of agreement. (There is a useful summary of this and the research in the NATE evidence to the Kingman Committee.)[1]

It is clear that children do not learn language as slavish imitators but as creative experimenters. From earliest infancy they are surrounded by adults who talk and use noises to soothe, control, amuse, and encourage them and, as soon as babies are able, they try out noises for themselves. What is interesting is the degree to which this process is led by the child's wishes and needs. When babies coo, adults coo back at them and use special kinds of words and noises in an attempt to make themselves understood by babies. Any little human without teeth is very likely to make a 'muh' or 'puh' sound as it opens its lips, or a 'tuh' or 'duh' sound with its tongue against its top gum. And all over the world, in all kinds of languages parents cry with delight, 'she said mama!' Whether the child intended to use such a word is not important. What is important is that the adults credit the baby with the intention, and do all they can to show pleasure and reinforce this word, by repeating it back to the child, encouraging the baby to make more sounds, building on this first step. And even before this stage, babies will have been lying awake in their cots, babbling and crooning the 'tunes' of the language, behaving like speakers of the language long before they are able to utter individual sounds.

Later on, when children start to use recognizable words like 'ball', they will use their few words to cover an enormous number of things, wishes and intentions, and adults will patiently try to discover what the child means, then smile and emphasize when they feel they have got it something like right. When a small child says, 'Daddy shoe', she might mean she wants daddy to put her shoes on her feet, that she wants him to play, to give him a present, or that she has seen her father's shoes, or ones like his, or that he should put them on. What adults do is try out various carefully selected expansions of 'daddy shoe' to see what the child is trying to say, on the correct assumption that the child has a rather larger passive vocabulary of words she can understand but not yet use. In doing so, of course, they are almost inadvertently teaching new words and patterns, or reinforcing ones the child will shortly be able to use for herself.

The same kind of process allows the child to work out the 'grammar' of the language. Children who have at one stage been using words like 'ran' and 'spoke' may suddenly start saying 'runned' and 'speaked' instead. This is not a mistake or going backwards. The children have become aware of the fact that they can tack '-ed' on to the ends of some words, to mean it is not happening now, and they are playing with it. By the time parents have become anxious, the child will have moved on, and be using 'ran' and 'spoke' again. From our point of view as teachers it is interesting to ask why these 'mistakes' do not persist, why the children self-correct, as it were. The answer seems to be that these forms do not get reinforcement from adults or slightly older children, so they fall away as children come to recognize the standard forms. It is interesting that the childish words which last longest are the ones children invent for themselves, which charm adults so much that they encourage children to perform them. When I asked a three-year-old in my street, 'What's your name, then?', she told me shyly, 'Dooby'. Since I knew her name was Lauren I asked her mum, who lives with her own parents and brothers. The mum blamed her family for saying so often to the little girl, 'Oh, *do* be quiet!', and when Lauren repeated it herself, her uncles had started using it as a pet name for her, so she had adopted it herself.

One other feature of children's early language learning deserves comment before we move on. Most of what I have been discussing so far could be described as informal and intuitive teaching, which many people would not recognize as teaching or instruction at all, a kind of 'sitting by Nellie' learning, assisted at best, though not inevitably, by a lot of love and encouragement. But many parents all over the world also teach their children language in a more formal sense, even though it arises just as much out of informal pleasure. It starts with a lullaby and little songs and develops into nursery rhymes, jingles and poems, often humorous and often woven around a game or actions which the child can join in. Parents have 'taught' their children such music and poetry since long before the invention of books, and long after it, often with only their own childhood memories to go on. It was not the popular songs of the 1940s that my mum sang to me as a child, but songs from the First World War.

Whatever the material they use, and whatever educational fashion demanded, parents seem to understand intuitively what Katherine Perera has recently stressed: the most important thing to learn about a language is the tune – the patterns, rhythms and cadences of the language. It should come as no surprise that poetry and song are the main vehicles for doing this, since for thousands of years the mnemonic devices of poetry – rhyme, rhythm, alliteration, assonance, etc. – have been used to enable humanity to recall and record when there were few other means of doing so. Even today it is commercial advertisers who most realise the power of these techniques with 'Beanz Meanz Heinz' or 'Coke is it'. Sadly, a great many primary and secondary teachers tend to avoid poetry with their pupils, perhaps because of their own experience as school pupils.

From this successful language learning experience it is possible to isolate some of the most significant features, a set of criteria against which to measure our own teaching.

1 The learning goes on largely inside children's heads where no one can 'see' it or control it, and the results of language learning may not be apparent to others

until some time later. In other words, competence precedes performance, often by some months.

2 It follows that children need to behave like speakers before they can actually speak in adult terms, to behave like readers or writers before they can do these things for themselves, and to behave like poets, novelists, reporters or dramatists too. In fact, it is mainly through this behaviour that children learn the important mental and conceptual structures which will eventually enable them to operate for real. It is a vital form of role-play.

3 Children learn through language as well as learning language itself and it gradually becomes an inextricable part of thinking and of personal identity. They are constantly adding to, expanding and modifying the world inside their heads by means of the language they encounter and the meanings they want to make. The initiative is therefore always the child's. Others can stimulate, interest and increase motivation, but can neither compel nor impose.

4 The driving force in children's language learning is *their* desire to take and make meaning, and to accomplish the things *they* want. Unless school learning can foster and develop this very powerful urge it will focus itself elsewhere.

5 Children learn language by using it, by trying things out and playing with words and expressions, thus gaining power and control over language. They cannot be 'given' language – they have to work it out for themselves, in a rich context where other language users provide models, examples and supportive help. This willingness in children to readjust and modify what they say and redraft or revise what they write is a matter of the confidence to take risks and make mistakes. It is very carefully fostered by parents, but easily discouraged by schools.

6 The most vital thing of all in children's early language learning is the almost unassailable expectation of parents that their children will become successful speakers of their mother tongue, they just take it for granted that it will happen and, barring physical impairment, it does. Countless studies have shown that teacher expectation is just as crucial, whether the teacher is aware of these expectations or not.

There is a fuller account of these criteria for successful language learning in David Allen's excellent booklet *English, Whose English?*.[3] Before I go on to discuss some of the implications of these criteria for primary and secondary classrooms I need to point up one of the essential features of successful language learning which I have left implicit. Language is by its very nature a social product, a symbolizing tool unique to human society, and its development is a byproduct of human interaction. Even highly literate adults need to make sense of things by talking about them, and talk and listening predominate in the learning experience of adults. Thought itself develops from talking to oneself and many important kinds of thinking are embedded in discussion.

A useful way of seeing the importance of this has been provided by Gordon Wells, in his adaptation of Roman Jakobson's model of how communication

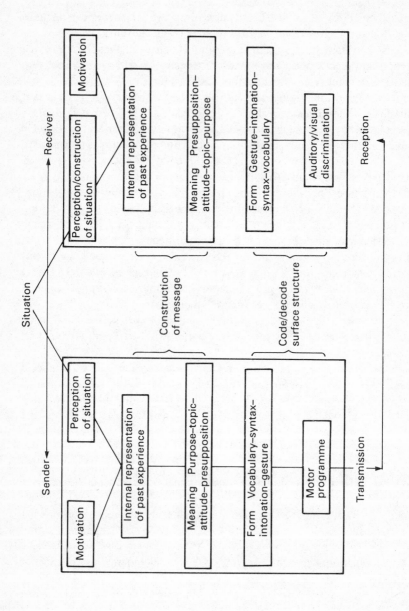

Figure 3.1 A model of the communication situation
After Wells (1976)[2]

occurs. It is clear from Figure 3.1 that there is no such thing as an active speaker and a passive listener: both are fundamentally reliant on each other, their shared social context, their assumptions about each other and the immediate feedback, often non-verbal, to each other. Readers need to learn how to reconstruct the missing speaker in order to replicate and engage in that process which we call reading, while writers need to learn how to reconstruct the missing listener or reader. Failure to be able to cotton on to these missing partners, to recreate the dialogue, is a bigger stumbling block to successfully attaining literacy than any of the more technical or mechanical aspects of either reading or writing.

As a simple example, if I say, 'the notes were sour because the seams were split', the difficulty with understanding is not the grammatical pattern, which is very familiar, or the meanings of the individual words. The problem is that it is a comment on the playing of bagpipes. In other words it is the social context in which words are used which to a large extent determines meaning. This interrelationship has been neatly summarized in the model of language offered by the National Association of Advisers in English in response to the Kingman Report.

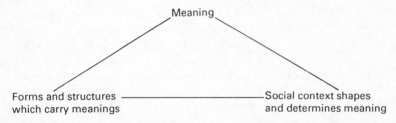

This I think puts the right emphasis on meaning, and it is also clear that all three are involved in language development and acquisition at all ages, for native speakers and potentially bilingual learners of English. Given the parity implied between social context and the forms and structures of the language it is also interesting to observe that no one attempts to teach school-age pupils anything about the social context of language use in any direct, systematic or comprehensive way. It just is. It is always and inextricably present as a shaping force, and we take it for granted that pupils progressively learn some of its effects and power, sometimes explicitly, sometimes not, and learn to take it into account through experience.

With the benefit of hindsight it is fairly easy to go back to the puzzle of my early fascination with particular kinds of exercises. What strikes me now as significant is that I liked finding new words and expressions and playing with them. Some aspects of this were common experience like talking and arguing and reading, others were more peculiar to me, because *I* happened to like games and puzzles. *First Aid in English*, so long as it was under my control and for my pleasure, appealed to me, and the same was probably true of poetry, too. I suspect that I temporarily lost my liking for either playing with words or reading and writing poetry because of top junior and lower secondary treatment of them. In short, someone highjacked the agenda, and made it part of a comprehensive and abstract system dominated by compulsion, obedience and 'right' answers, rather than part of my rhapsodic, intermittent, personal world.

I can remember poems like 'Look out, look out Jack Frost is about He's after your fingers and toes' which I picked up and remembered from my grand-mother's repetitions at the age of four, and many other poems from infant and junior years. But lower-school English is a complete blank, apart from having to copy out the whole of *King John and the Abbot of Canterbury* twice, because I got the margins wrong the first time. Which brings me to the implications for classroom teaching, both of my own learning as a youngster and what I have subsequently learned about language development from my teaching in primary and secondary schools.

First, I do not see how useful and permanent learning can occur without talk at any age. As a frequent visitor to primary and secondary classrooms these days I am worried by children working silently, unless they are all reading or actively watching or listening to something. This is particularly important when classes contain large numbers of bilingual learners who need as much discussion with other children as they can have, far more than they need to be reading or writing. The implication of what we have been saying about natural language learning is that children should be encouraged to work in pairs as soon as they are old enough to do so, discussing how to go about things, showing each other what they have done, helping each other to reflect, evaluate, redraft or have second thoughts when appropriate, and gossip when necessary. When larger groups are needed, pairs of pairs can work together.

It seems to me particularly important for children who are unlikely to engage much with what is called 'standard English' or school language outside school, for such children need a lot of experience of using English and hearing it over a number of years if they are not to see it as a challenge to their own language and identity and reject it as something belonging only to 'them'. I am not talking about local accents, or even dialect usage but the gradual acquisition of a wider repertoire of structural forms and vocabulary. Children need to feel comfortable with spoken forms, long before they will feel comfortable with them in reading and writing.

Second, in all aspects of our work we need to move further away from the right-answer syndrome towards terms that are more true and helpful – likely, unlikely, possible, probable, interesting, justifiable, more and less convincing, appropriate or whatever. This is particularly important when dealing with literature in all its forms for it is now clear that each reader brings almost as much meaning to a text as the writer was capable of putting into the black marks on the page. As Sterne put it in Tristram Shandy,

> . . . no author, who understands the just boundaries of decorum and good-breeding, would presume to think all: The trust respect which you can pay to the reader's understanding is to halve this matter amicably, and leave him something to imagine,

in his turn, as well as yourself. For my own part, I am eternally paying him the compliments of this kind, and do all that lies in my power to keep his imagination as busy as my own.[4]

In some areas of English work teachers both primary and secondary have understood this and made space for pupils' understandings and experiences of life and reading. Generally these are areas of profitable exploration which teachers and pupils have discovered for themselves. But other important aspects of English work have been much more resistant to this insight and they often involve those parts of the English curriculum and teaching approaches which were given a lot of attention when teachers were themselves pupils.

Prime among them is literature itself, which has not always been treated as Sterne would have wished, but as a vehicle for written or oral comprehension exercises, where through a teacher led class 'discussion' pupils were rewarded, demeaned or merely confused by the degree to which they were able to match the teacher's (or the crib notes) understanding of the text. This approach had a particularly damaging effect upon poetry, a form of writing often specifically designed to work at a variety of levels of intellect, logic, emotion or image, and to bear many rereadings and reconsiderations. There are more and less likely accounts, and more or less interesting or thought-provoking interpretations of poems; but there are no unambiguously 'correct' ones. A poem of Auden's such as 'Lay your sleeping head my love' is quite likely to be given an interpretation which is both unlikely and less interesting, if biographical details prove inconvenient.

Approaches which allow pupils to make their own connections and take their own time to reach an understanding of what the writer might have been trying to say are considerably more profitable than the competitive comprehension exercise type of approach. Hence the now widespread use of the strategies known as DARTS (directed activities related to texts), in which pairs of pupils are given a task which involves them in considering the text from a writer's point of view. Looking at an early or unpublished version of a text, for example, deciding what the writer may have been dissatisfied with, suggesting improvements themselves, then comparing suggestions with others in the class before considering the version finally published, can increase pupils' confidence in their own abilities and stimulate interest in the views and opinions of others. At best this will feed into their own writing as they realize that all writers make decisions about alternatives and what their readers may think or understand and that the choices we make on one day might well be different on another.

There is a huge range of such strategies which can be used profitably with both fiction and non-fiction texts right across the age range – making suggestions for missing or deleted words, predicting or sequencing activities, inventing interesting questions about the text, ranking statements or opinions as most or least agreed with, identifying the most exciting/boring/effective/moving/puzzling part of a text, adopting roles and critical standpoints and so on.

What interests me, quite apart from the freedom of imagination and inter-pretation which these approaches give to pupils, is the number of other benefits they entail. They capitalize on pupils' liking for solving problems and like many problems they admit of a variety of viable solutions. They enable *all* pupils in the class to be talking purposefully about language, life and literature, often at quite a high level. They encourage argument, persuasion, the use of evidence and reason, at an oral level and in quite a sustained way. And I would guess that inexperience in sustained argument of this kind is a better explanation of many pupils' difficulty with school or standard English, or with transactional writing, than their use of supposedly 'restricted' or 'elaborated' codes.

Somewhat paradoxically many teachers are now beginning to make use of such supporting structures to focus pupils' attention on language itself. Very young readers are quite capable of discussing the effects on meaning of different words and phrases. What is more surprising is to discover them just as readily talking about different word functions and sentence patterns, the grammatical and syntactical aspects and why one sentence might need to precede or follow another, how one arrangement might be more logical and another more striking or arresting. I would not want to oversell one particular group of strategies or teaching methods, for there are others which could be discussed, if space allowed.

I have simply been using them to illustrate what seems to me to be important general principles underlying a move towards a more natural and less didactic approach to learning about both language and literature. They are of a piece with a greater concentration on drafting and refining written work, much more frequent opportunities for pupils to talk and discuss, and a freer and more individual approach to reading, to literature and to media texts, without such constant reliance upon the analytic as the only mode of thought.

From this is being derived a much more open concern for children to learn what used to be called rhetoric – an awareness of the need for real audiences and real purposes for speech and writing, differences of form, style and function and of tone, effect and impact. Similarly, opportunities are being opened up for pupils to acquire useful terminology with which to discuss language and the way it works, including such matters as grammatical function, below and above the level of the sentence. The difference between past and present approaches to such matters is precisely one of order. Of course language is not some kind of symbolic verbal Lego, which children can be taught to assemble from being introduced to the various bits – drills, the naming of parts, and the bald primadonnas are what they always were: sterile, decontextualized and ineffective.

That is not, however, to say that such knowledge has no use, or even that it is irrelevant to pupils' increasing control and range as users of spoken and written language. The difference now is that many more teachers are aware of ways in which children's interest in language and the way it works can be stimulated, so that they can generate a climate in which pupils can express a need to know. Into such a climate it becomes possible to introduce appropriate terminology for things pupils are already aware of, and to develop their ideas about how to use language effectively.

A number of different things have helped us to reach this level of understanding. Perhaps most importantly, teaching classes with many bi- and multilingual pupils, with their in-built and intuitive awareness of difference and similarity in language, has created an open and natural context in which to discuss such matters across languages, and across dialects, varieties and styles of English. Techniques derived from drama teaching, utilizing children's gifts for imitation and mimicry, and teachers writing with and for children, have also helped; but so has word processing, by talking writing into the public and collaborative world of the visible screen, and in making writing much less laborious to alter, improve or simply move about the page. Last, increasing understanding of how language is acquired and develops, of the influence of social context upon the way language is used and understood, and the different approaches to text and media which modern critical theory have opened up, have helped to point us in the right direction.

This understanding concerns the one point of similarity I can see between language and Lego: whatever your starting point, you learn how to use it by playing with it. The more you can be encouraged to have fun with it, to use it to do what your inclination of fancy dictates to you, the more likely it is that you will develop the confidence to be able to play successfully and have games both amusing and serious.

Our job as teachers is not to provide pupils with a comprehensive and complete map of the way language is organized, even if such a thing existed. But neither is it to let them stumble blindly through this world without help or guidance. They have begun their own explorations long before they met us and will continue long afterwards. What we can do is share our knowledge, pleasure and experience with them and to stimulate their interest and curiosity in language and what it can do. We know things which will prove useful to them and we can devise situations which will enable them to discover things for themselves; we can supply names and ideas, and suggest strategies and objectives. What we cannot do is lay claim to all necessary or useful knowledge about language and literature, or route-march our pupils towards a set of predefined goals.

As with most good games, in playing with language there are many different ways of winning.

1   Exploring standard English in the classroom
CHRIS MARSHALL

A recent Scottish production of *As You Like It* had the autocratic court duke speaking standard English (SE) and the usurped duke seeking refuge in the forest with his band of merry men, speaking Scots. This shrewd directorial decision says much about language and power and is a useful starting point when considering the SE debate provoked by the two Cox reports. Contributors have tended to occupy one of three camps: the extreme right, subscribed to by the tabloids and Sheila Lawlor whose view is essentially 'Save the Queen's English'; the liberal middle grounders who broadly support Cox's compromise which acknowledges the equal status of non-standard dialects yet contends that the 'development of pupils' ability to understand written and spoken SE and to produce written SE is unquestionably a responsibility of the English curriculum'; and the radical left, represented by Cameron and Bourne who wryly extend Kingman's notion of SE as a 'great social bank' by arguing:

> What is not addressed is the issue of who put up the capital, who controls the means of linguistic exchange. We might well ask why it is that some people are forced to borrow at exorbitant rates of interest while their own currency lies valueless in a sock underneath in mattress![5]

The views of the English Working Group, essentially those of Michael Stubbs, have now been embodied in the statements of attainment and programmes of study for English in the national curriculum. Fearing a downpour of knowledge about language textbooks (Chapter 1: 'Capital letters'; Chapter 2: 'The full stop' . . . Chapter 36: 'Deixis'), I have experimented with different classroom approaches in an attempt to see what resources are most likely to open the SE 'pie' and what songs the birds will sing. Bearing in mind the pupil log books engendered by the learning about learning project and Cox's provision for Key Stage 3 that pupils 'should learn to use writing to facilitate their own thinking and learning' language logs became the vehicle for both the input materials and the pupils' responses. Working with eleven-, fourteen- and sixteen-year-olds in three different schools the format of the logs evolved during the project and provided fascinating insights into pupil attitudes towards language. I have left the quotations to speak for themselves.

Eleven-year-olds

The aim of the language log prototype was to foster a variety of exploratory talk and writing about accent, dialect, SE, context, the language of the community and the views of the English Working Group. The first of the several activities, spread over two or three hours' of lesson time, was for pupils to listen to a Scottish boy delivering his 'Five Lambies' class talk in Doric dialect with a very strong accent. Before and after log entries produced these responses:

> Before: I could not understand any of it, apart from the muff and fluff part. I think I could not understand most of it because he was speaking in a Scottish accent, and ever so quickly. When Scottish people speak, they often put words together, which makes it very hard to understand. He also had a bit of a croaky voice which made it harder as well.
>
> After: It was easier to understand after we had the words in front of us. Although it was easier, it was still hard to understand because he used words like 'wi'

instead of saying 'with', and 'tae' instead of 'to', but we decided it was not slang, just the way Scottish people speak.

(Claire)

Before: I understood quite a few things as some of it was in English, but some of it was in Scottish. I think it was about a boy who went out to a farm or something like that, did something with the animals, got mucky and when he went home he was sent to bed without any supper because he was dirty. This was hard to understand because he was talking Scottish and I don't speak Scottish. I did find that it did take a lot of listening to understand.

After: After we had listened to it three times and read it, I found it really quite easy to understand. As I had already got the gist of the story, I was able to try and translate the strange words he used to understand better, like 'loons' and 'quines' meaning male and female and so on. In this story he has different words for different things like we would use 'female' and he would use 'quines'. This sometimes can cause problems.

(Rachael)

Pupils then discussed and wrote about occasions when their own accents or syntax had been corrected:

I didn't used to sound the ends of my words and one of the ones I used to do a lot was wha(t) and I left the 't' off. My mum didn't like it because it was slang!

(Lucy)

At school the other day, I was doing some dancing and Louisa asked me who taught me it and I said 'Emma learnt me' and all my friends said 'you don't say she learnt me, you say she taught you'. If I say 'eh', my mum says 'say pardon'.

(Natasha)

Contrasting passages from *The Mayor of Casterbridge* and *The Family from One End Street* led to group talk, textual annotation and further class deliberations on the lexis and syntax of different region dialects while introducing the notion of linguistic and cultural stereotyping. Brief extracts from *Coronation Street* and *EastEnders* helped clarify the issues. The next activity, which proved the most challenging in its attempt to make explicit the implicit knowledge many pupils have, incorporated a Glaswegian/SE dialogue and invited pupils to 'define SE'.

I am not sure what Standard English is but I think it is words that you would find in a newspaper, radio, news broadcast or on *South Today* or any other TV news programme.

(James)

Standard English is not slang but not all perfect and posh. It is just normal general language.

(Tina)

It is a sort of language that nearly every person can understand and it is normal.

(Andrew)

I think that Standard English is mostly used by people who don't have much of an accent. Standard English is the normal way of talking English in a nice way.

(Clare S)

Standard English means to me that just ordinary people talk that way, not upper class people or common people. Just normal people talk that way. It is also not slang.

(Kelly)

The second half of the log shifted the emphasis from the nature of accent and dialect to the notion of context. Brief extracts from the Open University's *Every Child's Language*[6] inset pack stimulated reflection on 'which words don't fit' and why:

Lover: My dearest sweet, the cherished of my soul,
             My treasure-house of golden days in store,
             You give me pain, deeper than sword can thrust.
             The reason is . . . *you're standing on my flaming toe!*
It doesn't fit with what the person was saying at first.

Newsreader: Here is the news. There has been a serious case of assault in the House of Commons. Mr James Binks, the Minister for Underseas Development, was leaving the Chamber at the end of a debate, when a man, believed to be a journalist, approached him and gave him *a ruddy great kick up the pants.*
It is serious at first and at the end it sounds like a comedy.

Lecturer: The function of an electric bell is produced by electro-magnetic action. A two-pole electromagnet is energized and attracts the armature to which the hammer is attached. When contact is made, the circuit is at once broken, releasing the armature, so that the little hammer keeps waggling to and fro, in ever such a funny way. *And the little bell goes ting-a-ling-a-ling.*
This lecture sounds as though it is clearly written but at the end it does not sound like a scientist.

Through a simple drama activity groups of children then improvised the same scene 'caught in the act when "removing" ball-point pens from the school office . . .' in different contexts (pupil with teacher or parent or headteacher, etc.) paying particular attention to the contrasting language expectations. Two virtually blank log pages then asked on what occasions pupils would (a) speak and (b) write SE. Next, a simple questionnaire was devised to reveal that even in urban parts of West Sussex local vernacular flourishes:

In the area you live, how would you say the following things to a friend?

a) I am going to visit the park.
b) I am going to travel to Brighton.
c) Will you accompany me to the shops?
d) We'll take a short cut through this long, narrow gap between the houses.

The first question elicited these responses:

I'm going to the park

I'm going down the park.

I'm going to the rec.

I'm going along the park.

The final section of the log sought to widen pupils' thinking through contemplating the issues pondered by Cox himself: '"You should be able to talk and write how you want to." What are your reactions to this view?' Some pupils' reactions shamed the media's 'Sharon and Darren' level of analysis:

> I think we should because it is a part of our personality. So why should we change it?
>
> (Natasha)

> I think you should be able to speak how you want to because it is you. If you don't, it would not be you.
>
> (Tina)

> I think you should be able to talk and write how you want because if we all speak and wrote the same, it would be a boring world. And it's the way you speak so you should be able to speak yourself.
>
> (Claire)

> Yes we should be able to talk and write how we want to. If we learn a new way to talk, we could say things we don't mean.
>
> (Lucy)

Fourteen- and sixteen-year-olds

The log devised for older pupils retained the most successful parts of this format but attempted to refine the section asking pupils to define SE. This was expanded to include two accounts of the birth of Jesus:

> In the countryside close by there were shepherds who lived in the fields and took it in turns to watch their flocks during the night. The angel of the Lord appeared to them and the glory of the Lord shone round them. They were terrified, but the angel said, 'Do not be afraid. Listen, I bring you news of great joy, a joy to be shared by the whole people. Today in the town of David a saviour has been born to you; he is Christ the Lord. And here is a sign for you: you will find a baby wrapped in swaddling clothes and lying in a manger.'

> Nou i that same pairt the' war a wheen herds bidin thereout on the hill an keeping gaird owre their hirsel at nicht. Suddent an angel o the Lord cam an stuid afore them, an the glorie o the Lord shined about them, an they war uncolie frichtit. But the angel said tae them: 'Dinna nane afeared: I bring ye guid news of gryte blytheness for the haill fowk – this day in Dauvit's Toun a sauviour hes been born til ye Christ the Lord! This d gate ye s'ken it is een as I say: ye will finnd a new born bairn swealed in a barrie an liggin intil a a heck'.

After discussion, tentative definitions of SE were again attempted and this time round were measured against my own equally tentative definitions of dialect and SE, supported by a simple linguistic map showing how East Midlands dialect became the language of wider communication. The second adjustment was the inclusion of an example from *The Linguistic Atlas of England*[7] and a related task. Equipped with the knowledge that in the 1950s there were at least 45 regional versions of words for 'snack' (from 'bagging' to 'tommy'), pupils were given pages from the atlas and asked to analyse the variations and assess what they revealed about language:

> I think this task has proved to me that there are more than three different dialects.
>
> (Ian)

> Why do people have different accents and words for donkey?   (Declan)

> That people use different words for the same meanings, and that the way you talk shows what group of people come from, and that no one talks proper English – just what they think it is.   (Claire)

Sixteen-year-olds had *The Family from One End Street* replaced by an extract from Toni Cade Bambara's *Gorilla, My Love*[8] and were asked in pairs to examine a range of poems written in non-standard English: Scottish, Dorset, Caribbean, Yorkshire, etc. In the light of their analysis, they were asked to talk and write in their logs about this proposal from the *Penguin Book of Caribbean Poetry*:[9]

> The obvious danger of self-isolation by too extreme a use of the vernacular, however authentic, when the whole of the English-speaking world awaits as a potential audience, have to be balanced against the loss of that unique cultural identity which can result from exclusive use of Standard English.

Typical responses were:

> I believe that the use of regional accents adds character and diversity which would be lost by universal Standard English. The cultural identity is just as important as the majority's view of how the English language should be spoken . . .
>
> When the dialect is written, if successful, it is almost as important as visual elements in setting the atmosphere. The character is very important and it leaves Standard English . . . sounding quite bland and uninteresting.
>
> (Sarah)

> Both are important, but powerful groups in society consider one to be more important than another. It also depends on the context of what is written and who is writing in 'standard' English, then some of the meaning is lost.
>
> (Peter)

John Agard's suggestion that 'Our use of language is a subversive activity but to subvert is often to enrich' stimulated discussion of the relationship between language and power[10], supported by Jimi Rand's 'Talk, Talk: Nigger Talk Talk'[11] and Tony Harrison's 'The Queen's English'[12]. Finally, 'Should school pupils be encouraged to speak and write SE?'

> I think that school pupils should be encouraged to speak and write Standard English, to allow them to be understood by the majority of English people. Yes, I think that their ability should be tested as it would be to their advantage to be able to communicate with the majority of English people – allowing them positions of work, communication etc. outside of their locality.

However, in saying this, I still believe their local dialect should still be taught so that history won't die out and they can still retain some of their traditions, etc.

(Sharon)

I think that school children should not be encouraged to speak and write Standard English. Some people may believe that it is important for young children to learn the 'proper' way of talking and writing but I do not. Children should be able to talk in their local dialect without being thought of as unnatural. This will happen if children are expected to speak the same. Children should not grow up with these prejudices against others.

Not only would it cause some children to be 'picked on', the use of Standard English might lead to the demise of many local dialects.

I also believe that they should not be tested on their ability to speak and write Standard English. Many people who already have learning difficulties would find it almost impossible to do well in such a test, as it would be unnatural to them. It would also mean the loss of many 'nice' accents, and mean that to me, it would seem 'boring' if everyone spoke the same way.

(Stephanie)

Although a good solid grasp of the English language and the way it is spoken is essential for all pupils, I do not believe school pupils should be encouraged to speak and write Standard English. This would lead to many dialects being forgotten and a lot of history and information on pockets of society being lost forever. The encouragement to speak and write Standard English would just lead to a further centralisation of society towards the south-east of England, coming mainly from areas with their own distinct dialects: Wales, Scotland, Yorkshire, the Black Country etc. etc . . . 'know what I mean'. Testing should take place, but only relative to their locality.

(Jim)

Where does this leave us?

1 There is a need to experiment with language resources and refine them through experience. Teachers will need to draw on a range of resources, particularly those contained within the pupils and community, rather than hope to discover the definitive, all-encompassing 'pack'.

2 'Writing can have cognitive functions in clarifying and supporting thought': children need to reflect on language through tentative information writing as well as through talk. Language logs provide one vehicle for this.

3 Children know far more about language than we often realize but find some issues, such as defining SE, more conceptually demanding and consequently more challenging to comment on explicitly. It is important that this area is properly researched and resourced.

4 Linguistic prejudice is rife: in families, classrooms and, regretfully, some staffrooms. However, well informed teachers, aided in the long term by the Language in the National Curriculum (LINC) project, are able to counteract this and the English Programmes of Study (POS) legitimize this.

5 Literature is a vital component in facilitating exploration of language issues. It

is a matter of regret that Cox II did not place greater emphasis on the potential of non-standard texts to illuminate the advantages and disadvantages of writing in either standard or non-standard forms and as a means of exploring language and power. Early statements by Ron Carter's LINC project recognize that: 'Language reveals and conceals much about social relationships. There is an intimate connection between language and social power, language and culture and language and gender.'

Clearly LINC have the ideal opportunity to put literature at the centre of language exploration. Returning to the Forest of Arden, we need to remain aware that:

> Discussing language and how it works with school pupils . . . would need to include the fact that no discussion of appropriateness can be honest if it does not ask who are the arbiters of what is appropriate and who confers on them their powers.

2 Eight- and nine-year-olds getting to know about language
NIKKI SIEGEN-SMITH

Wilson Primary School is on the edge of the centre of Reading where children speak over twenty different languages and reflect the diversity and richness of our multiethnic society.

We have a shared philosophy of children's learning and a collegiate approach to decision making. It is within this framework that we plan to work through whole school projects. We have a cycle of themes which we hope ensures continuity and progression and an entitlement curriculum for each child.

During our 'languages' project, the issues of Kingman and 'knowledge about language' (KAL) were just beginning to emerge. It was an exciting time to explore what that meant for children in the classroom. It became increasingly interesting to examine those contexts which we had frequently used to promote children's learning to see whether they could be contexts for promoting knowledge about language.

But what is KAL? Was it just those 'small bits' about adjectives, verbs and nouns or was it the bigger bits, the macro factors – how does writing behave? Who is an audience? How do books work? What are the features of print? Who speaks when – to what purpose and why? What can language do for you? What does it mean to be bilingual? Why do people sound different? What are scripts? Letters? and how does modern technology fit in?

Our project had new starting points, established procedures and the children's own resourcefulness and enthusiasm. We invited the parents in to tell stories in English and mother tongues. We collected old writing implements; made our own inks and had lessons in Chinese characters. We had a book week, published.

our own books to read to each other and made pop-up books for a member of our family. We conducted a language survey across the whole school and coordinated the research. We sought out greetings in as many languages as possible and used them. We continued with our silent reading, book sharing, book interviews – handwriting sessions and opportunities to write for a variety of purposes. We continued to take books home to share with our families and to speak to peers and adults in small groups and large assemblies.

Our environment continued to be one which promoted learning. We had fabrics, books and displays at every turn; our furniture was arranged to facilitate class discussions, group discussions, work in pairs and independently. We hoped that our relationships policy pervaded our school: one of mutual trust, openness, welcome and the valuing of each individual.

It was obvious that KAL was knowing about full stops and capital letters – but it was also about those huge questions – what is my language – and what does it do for me?

It was also obvious that our project, which contained both new starting points and established procedures, a school philosophy for the environment and relationships and new ways of doing things, could also be a context for developing KAL.

When we spent several days learning from Choon's dad how to write Chinese characters we learned that writing could take a variety of forms. The children interacted with a visiting adult and with each other. They discussed the differences between Cantonese script and English. They also began to make connections with other bilingual texts available in the classroom – discovering Urdu, Russian and Amharic (Kingman on historical and geographical variation: 'As populations are dispersed and separated, they typically develop regular regional changes in their language forms' (p. 30, Figure 5)).[13]

When Asher's mum came to read us poems from John Agard's *I Din Do Nuttin*[14] you could see the pride in the black children's eyes. Asher's mum sat there on the chair and read us poems that reminded her of her own childhood. We could have listened for hours. Asher took over where her mum left off and taught me how to read the one about the alligator:

Don call alligator scissor mout
Till you cross de river

In front of us existed living proof, through our excitement of the poems, of 'the ways in which historically and currently groups settling in Britain have enriched English' (Kingman, p. 30).

Then the children made books for a member of their family. Who for? What kind of illustrations? What size of print? How accurate the punctuation? Should there be spelling mistakes? What should the cover be? Should the author's name be on the front? Julie designed hers for her baby sister: a beautiful pop-up book with illustrations to go with her sister's favourite nursery rhymes. (Kingman,

Summary, Figure 2: 'Speakers and writers adapt language to the context in which the language is being used').

Julie knew about authors, illustrations and that 'baby sister' language was different from language for dads who loved reading about football (Richard was using that type of language for his book for his dad).

Gareth was in the group which was experimenting on which substances produced the best inks. Was it the blackberries or the onion skin? It was part of the task to write up the process of ink making. The purpose of the writing was twofold: to help Gareth organize his thoughts and to use his description as a 'recipe' for somebody else to have a go. We talked explicitly about how it would help him to organize his thoughts. It was well worth discussing this aspect of his work. Gareth began to know the power of language to organize. ('Language is the instrument of intellectual development'; Kingman, p. 8, Chapter 2.10).

Our project led us to discuss, to argue, to compromise, to role play, to share ideas, to convince and to communicate. The role of the teacher was to develop the environment, the relationships and the context in which to make explicit knowledge about language with children.

Towards the end of the project we discussed language in an overt way. These are some of the things the children said:

> I think um you can use language for sending messages on phones.
>
> (Clive)

> When people ask you about yourself, you can answer them, you can ask things, you can make friends.
>
> (Choon)

> I think you can use language for talking to people and using your brain so that you can think up things.
>
> (Steven)

> You can use your language for if you go to a different country and the people in that country don't understand English say . . . you could use another language.
>
> (Kerry)

> I use writing for sending messages to people in other countries. I send letters to Jamaica and Canada . . . With writing you don't have to be there to say something.
>
> (Clive)

> You can use writing for sending postcards. I think you can also use writing for newspapers. I think you can use it for poems as well. I like poems when they rhyme. Sometimes poems tell me what things are like, like what the sea is like.
>
> (Mandy)

> I think about writing that it learns me a lot. It teaches me about people. My best thing about writing was when I wrote about dressing up as Winnie the Pooh. My writing reminds me of that.
>
> (Steven)

It seems increasingly apparent that a curriculum which focuses on language in action enables Mandy, Choon, Rebecca and Clive to develop a growing knowledge *about* language.

3   Knowledge about language through the curriculum

PAUL RHODES

Imagine a ring of pupils standing in a drama studio. They have been told that they can sit down whenever they like but the lesson will not start until everyone is sitting down. After twenty minutes five increasingly beleaguered pupils are subjected to a variety of taunts: 'Sit down you're wasting our drama time'; 'Come on, you've proved you're macho'. In subsequent discussion it was fascinating to see how pupils used language individually at first and then as part of a pressure group. The type of language generated arose out of a need to change other people's behaviour in order to satisfy their own needs and desires. Now imagine an irate, tired householder trying to dissuade an over-zealous British Telecom engineer who wants to install a telephone kiosk in the living room of a semidetached in an attempt to preempt vandalism or a pupil walking into a greengrocer's and asking for a kilo of elephants! Drama lessons provide good opportunities to look at face to face communication and study the many non-verbal forms such as proxemics and kinesics, or take just one channel of communication such as pitch or facial expression and slowly build by adding other forms such as gesture and posture.

It is important to begin with an account of work undertaken outside of the English classroom because, of course, pupils use language in all subject areas not just in English. This fact has been reinforced by visits to other classrooms and complemented by cross-curricular approaches facilitated by the school's participation in the national oracy project under whose aegis we have been able to investigate interaction in the classroom, small-group discussion and the use of subject-specific vocabulary. I was invited to join forces with the head of science who wanted to use more talk in her laboratory. We planned a jigsaw on how the computer has changed our daily lives. Pupils were allocated expert groups in which they discussed different ramifications of the task such as how leisure might be affected or the impact of micro-technology upon the home. The same pupils would then go to different groups and contribute their newly acquired expertise in a discussion focusing on the more global aspects of the problem. The resulting success of this experiment meant that far more talk-based activities were attempted both within the science department and elsewhere as others were eager to achieve similar results.

The benefit to the English department means that we no longer have to induct pupils into the whys and wherefores of constructive talk and department practice is reinforced in other subject areas. In English pupils are encouraged to experiment and reflect on their use of language at different levels. *Understanding Language* by Katherine Perera[15] has been used as an 'A' level coursework text and in the lower school pupils have worked on assignments looking at how the indices of race, gender and status affect their use of language. During the autumn term the fifth years do a work experience project; as a part requirement they all record their impressions and observations on language-related aspects – types of communication used in the workplace; awareness of context-specific language; how hierarchy and position dictate form and content, the use of body language, etc. This raw data is then brought back to the classroom and processed within small groups during which several oral assessments are made and one unit is completed for the LEAG dual accreditation English syllabus. Now the GCSE has vindicated the importance of talk in the classroom it has replaced writing as the main focus of activity. The reduced demands of the new courses have meant that we are able to spend far more time on preparatory work for assignments so each one takes about three weeks to complete from talk to final draft. This has resulted in a more in-depth approach to text work and language awareness assignments and it has given more opportunities for pupils and teachers to intervene during the different stages of the process and hence the dialogue between reader and writer has been strengthened.

In media studies denotative/connotative analyses allow pupils to examine the rhetorical uses of the camera. Pupils enjoy using a new language which indexes their own expertise in a hitherto unknown area of experience. Tracking shots, diagonal composition and chiaroscuro are words and phrases which indicate a new found confidence in an ability to use language within a limited context. Having acquired a familiarity with technical terminology the children are able to manipulate the language of the image to make their own statements about the world. Parents have commented that watching *Eastenders* or *Cagney and Lacey* will never be the same again as they are given running commentaries on camera position, point of view shots and symbolic references.

The Head of Craft Design and Technology is a member of the oracy project working group and he invited me to judge and offer comments upon the process of designing and constructing a menu holder. Third-year pupils were encouraged to use precise language when giving their expositions and to be aware of the type of audience to whom they were speaking. This exercise highlighted the need to examine the latent ambiguity of everyday words such as perpendicular, true and horizontal. It was quite clear that these words were being used in very different ways. As a result all staff were invited to answer a questionnaire which asked for their own common-sense definitions of a list of twenty words. Now staff are much more aware of the language that they are using and they do not assume a common understanding on the part of the pupils.

Visits to other classrooms have been very revealing. As English teachers we often arrogantly assume that we are the only staff concerned with the mechanics of language usage. It was quite a salutary experience to find that some of the best language work was being done in other areas; my prejudices took a severe knock!

4   Tuning up: what one professional writer needs to know about language

PHILIP PULLMAN

I am writing about tuning up from a writer's point of view: from the perspective of someone who spends most of his time writing stories and getting paid for them (stories both for the page and for the TV screen). What I know about language, and about tuning up, if it makes a difference at all, makes a difference to my ability to pay the mortgage this month. So my relationship with language is not only a tuning-up one, it is also that of farmer and cow. I try to keep the beast contented and well so that she will give plenty of milk. It is instrument as well, of course: I play on it, and pass the hat round.

Recently I have been trying to become conscious of what part my knowledge about writing plays in my work. I know the attainment targets pretty well, and I have to say at the outset that there is very nearly nothing in them of the slightest relevance or use to what I do every day. For instance, the need to hear what I write. After I'd written the first paragraph of this, I read it through aloud, as my habit is, as a check against errors. Needing to *hear* what I have written says something about my – not so much knowledge as experience of language. I have found over many years that I cannot write when there's music playing because the rhythm gets in the way. One reason why writing prose is harder than writing verse is that you have to be especially attentive to the rhythm. Without a metre to rely on, you have to hear the rhythm clearly in order to make your paragraphs move instead of sitting like fat lumps on the page. Music makes it impossible. I can write not happily but perfectly well when there's a lot of traffic noise, or when people are talking, or when there's a pneumatic drill digging up the road outside; but the faintest thread of music from the limits of audibility makes writing very difficult. Rhythm underlies everything. Quite often – and that last sentence is a case in point – I know how long the next sentence is going to be, or whether it is going to break into three chunks or two, before I even know what it is going to say. I hear what the rhythm wants to do and try to find words to fit it.

Here is an exercise which illustrates that, and tunes you in to the rhythm of prose. Take a sentence – any sentence – and try to duplicate its rhythm exactly in another sentence using different words. It is easy to do it just by repeating the shape and substituting one word for another of the same sort (my sister tickles the cat; her brother buried the dog). But if you can do it by varying the grammatical structures as well, so much the better.

Here's an example (from Dorothy Wordsworth's *Journal*): 'After tea we walked to Butterlip How and backwards and forwards there.' You could duplicate it like this:

'By the way, we had to cancel the milk, because of the holiday.' Or like this:

'Bernard Shaw was wearing leaves in his hair and driving a Cadillac.'

It does not matter if it is nonsense as long as it makes sense. (I wonder if you could say that sentence in any other language than English?)

It is more difficult than it looks. Even harder is to take not just one sentence but an entire paragraph and try to duplicate the rhythm of that. And harder still is to make them work consecutively, as a story, say. You will not make any money doing it but it is fun and it is all part of tuning up.

What I am getting at is that the knowledge about language of which I am conscious when I write is something beyond, or behind, or beneath those attainment targets in the Kingman and Cox reports. I am faced with quite different problems from those which a knowledge of the difference between statements and questions, for example, would solve. Or even a knowledge of the rules of spelling. (That tickles me. At seven in Kingman there are rules; at eleven there are regularities; at sixteen there are not even regularities. It's like a sort of mystery religion – as the neophytes get older, they're gradually initiated into the secret that there's *nothing there* behind the veil.)

Here is one problem from real life. What do you do when you do not know what to write next? The story is stuck. You are stuck. Do you wait for inspiration? Amateurs are very fond of inspiration. They attribute miracles to it; they think that professionals are people who are more inspired than they are, and that if only they were inspired every day, they might be professionals too. And there is the sentimental Bohemian idea that being inspired is like being drunk and you can find inspiration in alcohol or marijuana. The truth about inspiration is that it comes when you are stone cold sober and bored stiff, having sat and stared at the same wall for hours. And a professional is simply someone who can write just as much without being inspired. So what do you do when you are stuck? What do you do when there is a blank page in front of you, a deadline ahead of you, and a bank manager very close behind you?

Do the attainment targets tell us?

Well, here's Raymond Chandler's answer. When in doubt, he said, 'have a man come through the door with a gun'. Golden words, which I have got pinned up above my desk. Believe me, it works.

Here is another problem. Where do you tell the story from? Where is the narrating consciousness located? Another way of putting the question is to ask how many minds you are going to take readers into. And what are you going to let them see when they are there? This, to my mind, is the most difficult and fascinating problem of all, and one which you face with fresh intensity each time you begin a new story. There is no time to go into all the implications now, but it is something which attainment targets do not make you aware of. You only come up against this when you do it – when you write a story. And your awareness of the problem sharpens your reading no end.

Here's another. You are describing a scene and you want to bring it to life. What do you know about language that will help you do that?

In a book I wrote called *The Ruby in the Smoke*,[16] which is set in the Victorian East End, a little girl, Adelaide, is lighting an opium pipe for a sailor.

He did as the little girl said, stretching out languorously on his side. The chilly grey light of the fading afternoon, struggling through the grime on the tiny window, gave the scene the sombre colour of a steel engraving. An insect crawled lethargically across the greasy pillow as Adelaide applied a lighted match to the lump of opium. She passed the drug, transfixed on a pin, to and fro across the flame until it began to bubble and the fumes soaked outwards. Bedwell sucked at the mouth-piece; and Adelaide held the opium above the bowl, and the sweet heady smoke was dragged into the pipe.

When it had stopped smoking, she lit another match and repeated the process. She hated it. She hated what it did to him, because it made her think that under every human face there was the face of a staring, dribbling, helpless idiot.

'More,' he mumbled.

'There ain't no more,' she whispered.

'Come on, Adelaide,' he whined. 'More.'

'One more then.'

Again she struck a match; again the opium bubbled and fumed. The smoke poured into the bowl like a river disappearing underground. Adelaide shook out the match, and dropped it with its fellows on the floor.

Now one of the things I know about language is that words colour each other, and you can make a word do more work than the grammar appears to allow it to. Why did I say steel engraving and not just engraving? Or why not copper engraving? Most engravings are on copper, after all, and they print the same colour as steel ones. But steel is grey and copper is not. I wanted a grey colour in the reader's mind. Take the word transfixed. It applies to the little lump of sticky opium on its pin; it also, of course, colours our understanding of the little girl at her task, and more especially, of the sailor, watching her, hypnotized by what she's doing. Transfixed. The meaning of the word soaks outwards a little way as we read. It colours the sentences next to it. Take the word insect. That word breaks a rule, which is to be as precise as you can. I could have said bedbug or cockroach or fly; why did I say insect? Because at that moment our attention is the sailor's attention – it is concentrated intensely on the opium. We see the insect, as it were, out of the corner of the eye. Take the last sentence but one. Language has echoes. One reader in a thousand might catch the echo in this: the echo of another river that disappears underground, the echo of another experience with opium. Coleridge, of course: 'Kubla Khan'. I do not really care if it is only one reader in ten thousand, because the image works on the visual level for everyone else: you do not shortchange people by giving them good stuff.

Most of my professional life is concerned with the making of stories. Now you do not need language to tell stories; one of the most vivid experiences of my life – simultaneously uplifting and lowering – was watching a performance by the mime group Theatre de Complicité four or five years ago. They were telling stories which were perfectly comprehensible, stories with layers of meaning, stories with irony and humour and wit, without using a single word. Suddenly I felt that my knowledge about language was redundant. Here was somebody doing what I tried to do, and doing it very well, but not using my tools. Another illustration of that can be found in an odd little book called *Passionate Journey*, by Frans Masereel, first published in 1919. It is a novel – I do not know what else you could call it – and it is told entirely in pictures, in very expressionist woodcuts. You can follow the story, and it is a moving one, and you do not read a single word. You do not need to.

But then I saw that the Theatre de Complicité, and Frans Masereel, and for that matter Charlie Chaplin, are operating as I do beneath, behind, beyond language, beyond the level where you set up attainment targets and measure things. But that is the place where stories come from, and whether they come out in pictures or in words is a secondary question. I am thinking all the time of what I am conscious of as I write. I do not think about – for instance – the distribution of subject noun phrases in my sentences; I do think about the shape of the story. Every story has a shape. You find that out when you try to tell it. You find that there is a pure line – imaginary, like the Greenwich meridian, like the equator – going through the centre of the story. It is your job as the storyteller to find that line and then cleave as closely to it as you can.

To illustrate that: I have just spent two years trying to get a novel started properly. In September I thought I had it and I raced through till about page 175, and then my sense of things not quite working became too strong to ignore, so I stopped and examined it. And it was clear what I had done wrong. Characters were spending a lot of time sitting around telling each other things or accidentally coming across articles in the newspaper which told them things, or finding letters which revealed things – and it was all because I had started in the wrong place. That pure line going through the story: I had started too far along it. So I scrapped what I had done, began the novel again six months later and so far – touch wood – it is all right. Is that a matter of knowledge about language? It's certainly a matter of tuning in to the sense of story – and you do not get tuned in to that unless you *do* it.

There is a great deal more I could say about this story-telling business, and particularly about the relationship between words and pictures, which is exercising me at the moment both because I am writing the words for a picture book and because I am adapting *Ruby* for television. I would like to say something, following Frank Smith's very useful notion of the literacy club (which we can all join), about the picture-making club from which most of us are excluded because of no talent, no confidence, no technology. How much of children's experience of story these days comes from the TV screen? The vast bulk of it. And it is not the language that carries most of the meaning – it is the pictures. And can we duplicate this? No, we cannot. Anyone – in one sense – could write *Ulysses*; you just need a pen and paper. However, you couldn't put *The Singing Detective* or *Dr Who* together without a million pounds or more, actors, technicians, designers, a technology and a bureaucracy. And it is no good looking at the script; the script is not the experience. There is a picture-making club from which most of us, including in many cases the scriptwriter, will always be excluded, and that is worth examining.

I would also like to examine the question of whether the Latin I learned from the age of eight has made any difference to my awareness of whether, for instance, a sentence works or whether it does not. I feel that it has; but it is too far down, too deeply embedded, too much a part of me, for me to be able to take it out and pretend not to have it. So are the rhythms of the Book of Common Prayer, large chunks of which I inattentively acquired by heart. I am curious to know what it would be like without them, but I doubt whether I ever shall.

And there is a great deal more to be said about children's own writing, and why they are better at dialogue than they are at narrative. There is a great deal to be said about the Kingman and Cox reports – but not by me – though I would like to express my regret at the obsessive concentration on writing in the attainment targets, given what HMI and the APU have said, and what we all know, about the amount of writing children already do. It is like that little boy on his first day at school. He came out and his mummy was waiting at the gate and she said 'Hello, darling! Did you have a nice day at school? What did you learn?'

'I learned to write', he said.

'Oh, darling, you learned to write! That's wonderful! What did you write?'

'I dunno', he said. 'I can't read.'

And finally, I realize that I have come to the end of this piece and I have not mentioned the parts of speech. So here is something just to show that you have not wasted your time in reading this. Take a story (and tell your pupils to do it too) like Cinderella or Little Red Riding Hood, which they know well, and write it out in exactly a hundred words. Not one more, not one less. They will say they cannot do it, but they will manage it, with some trimming and cutting and fiddling. Then they read them out and they are all wonderful, and you tell them that they are so good that the fairy godmother has given them an extra five words to use as they like. And if you want to, you can seal a prediction in an envelope, and when they've put in their extra five words you can unseal it and it will say 'Most of the extra words will be adjectives, and some will be adverbs.' And they will. If they do not know the term adjective, you can use this to show them what it means, and if they do, you can point out something about adjectives, which is that they are not essential – they have just managed to tell the story without them, after all; but they are the most useful of the luxuries.

And it will also sharpen the children's sense of story shape; in a hundred words, you have to tell the story and nothing but the story and you have to get it right. I believe strongly in *getting it right*. Tuning up, after all, implies that there is a state when things are out of tune and that it is possible to make an adjustment which will get them in tune: getting it right. But my understanding of *getting it right* has nothing to do with attaining targets; it has much more to do with milking that cow, or playing that instrument.

Notes

1 M. Barrs *et al.* (1988) *Evidence to the Committee of Inquiry into the Teaching of English Language*, NATE.

2 G. Wells (1976) 'Comprehension: what it means to understand', *English in Education*, vol. 10, no. 2.
3 D. Allen (1988) *English, Whose English?*, National Association of Advisers in English.
4 L. Sterne (1967) *The Life and Opinions of Tristram Shandy, Gentleman* London: Penguin (written 1759–1767).
5 D. Cameron and J. Bourne (1989) *Grammar, Nation and Citizenship: Kingman in Linguistic and Historical Perspective*, Institute of Education, University of London.
6 Open University (1985) *Every Child's Language* (Course P534), Milton Keynes: Open University Press.
7 H. Orton *et al.* (1978) *The Linguistic Atlas of England*, New York: Croom Helm.
8 T. C. Bambara (1984) *Gorilla, My Love*, London: The Women's Press.
9 P. Burnett (ed.) (1986) *The Penguin Book of Caribbean Verse*, London: Penguin.
10 J. Elkin and P. Triggs (1986) *The Books for Keeps Guide to Children's Books for a Multi Cultural Society 8–12*, London: Books for Keeps.
11 J. Berry (1984) *News for Babylon: The Chatto Book of West Indian British Poetry*, London: Chatto & Windus.
12 T. Harrison (1984) *Selected Poems*, London: Penguin.
13 DES (1988) *Report of the Committee of Inquiry into the Teaching of English* (Kingman Report), London: HMSO.
14 J. Agard (1983) *I Din Do Nuttin & Other Poems*, London: Bodley Head.
15 K. Perera (1987) *Understanding Language*, Manchester National Association of Advisers in English.
16 P. Pullman (1985) *The Ruby in the Smoke*, Oxford: Oxford University Press.

PART FOUR
Writing

4 Shifting emphases

PAT D'ARCY

In the past two decades there have been many interesting developments in the field of writing. As a result, what children write, how they write and the expectations that they and their teachers bring to writing have all changed, sometimes quite dramatically. It goes without saying that in some classrooms the scene is still much as it has always been but overall there have certainly been some clearly discernible shifts of emphasis.

The most significant shift, to which the National Curriculum Council has now given full support, is the shift from correctness to composition – from regarding writing primarily as a secretarial skill to regarding the act of writing as a powerful mental process. In the same way that reading is now recognized by many teachers as an active engagement of the reader with the text in which meaning is brought to the words and pictures on the page in order for meaning to be made from them, so writing has come to be recognized not simply a matter of learning the code or even the various forms that written language can take, but first and foremost as a meaning-shaping activity in which the writer's thoughts and feelings are made visible as the marks are made on page or screen.

There are several implications of this shift from the importance in the first instance of 'getting it right' to the importance of discovering what the 'it' might be. Strategies are now being developed by teachers to help children draw more deeply on their own stored experience as a starting point for further exploration in their writing. There is a more widespread recognition that although writing is helping the writer to shape meaning this rarely happens all in one go. The writer can be encouraged to see her writing taking shape through various stages – exploratory, draft, revision, with a freedom to make changes which in the past was often denied or ignored. From time to time the writer can pause to share her thoughts with the teacher or with a friend about the ideas or the recollections that are emerging. In this respect writing need no longer be a solitary act of endurance although children committed to meaningful writing will often persist for longer and produce more.

Clearly the teacher's role has shifted in emphasis also, from that of arbiter to helper, interested more in responding helpfully to work in progress than in 'marking' writing with which there has been no previous direct contact. More frequently now in both primary and secondary classrooms, teachers write when their pupils do, especially in the exploratory stage prior to any continuous drafting. It is easy for everyone to join in a five-minute brainstorm designed to recollect initial data about people or places or factual information or a sequence of 'pictures in the mind'. Everyone's first thoughts can then be shared, talked about, added to.

If a joint topic is about to get under way, the next stage could be to brainstorm again for questions – what *do* you not know about . . . so that mini-investigations can be started to find out more through reading, talking to people, writing down what has been discovered, coming back to share, reconstruct, build a more coherent picture together. In this way writing as part of the learning process becomes one mode of expression among many rather than a task to be pursued for its own sake. The teacher can help to coordinate, can share the investigating, the talking and the writing up, becoming more aware of individual strengths and weaknesses through her own active participation.

Where the writing is not focused on a joint class activity, teachers who put composing first will encourage free writing to help ideas or memories to flow, will help children to find a focus which will lead them confidently into a draft and will remind them that there will be time for checking spellings, etc., at the looking back, proof-reading stage but that capturing their own thoughts and feelings must come first. This is not to abandon a concern for correctness but to fit it into its appropriate place: at the revision stage once the words are there and can receive the writer's full attention. Trying to compose and edit simultaneously is a soul-destroying task which has turned many adults as well as children into unconfident writers.

The effects of this shift from viewing writing predominantly as code to viewing it predominantly as composition can be seen most dramatically in the spread over the past few years of 'emergent writing' in infant classrooms. Thanks to the widespread dissemination made possible by the national writing project more and more teachers have become interested in giving even the youngest children ownership of their own writing from their first day in school. Researchers like Clay and Graves were showing in the late 1970s how confidently young children will approach writing if they are encouraged to invest their earliest marks with meaning.

Teachers have rapidly found out for themselves that four- and five-year-olds can indeed represent the thoughts they hear in inner speech inside their heads as marks on paper. Even at the prephonic stage, 'scribble' writing is definitely not scribble thinking! Thus from the start children can use their own writing as an act not merely of copying but of composition. Teachers turning the child's writing into adult writing, so that the child can learn about the differences without releasing ownership of her own thoughts, can start the child off as a confident meaning maker. This shift still has considerable potential if only it were followed through consistently from five to fifteen and beyond.

Furthermore, the same strategies for meaning making in 'stages' that are used with older children can just as well be used with infants. It is just as easy to brainstorm a list of words about 'snow' or 'Christmas' or 'the seaside' as it is to make up a complete sentence – and the potential of ideas in a list is often far greater than 'Snow is cold' or 'I like the seaside'. A list will contain more meaningful words which can be talked about, and then each of them expanded in the child's own writing. Pupils of all ages can often be helped in the exploratory stage by drawing first and then talking about or writing on their drawings – not the definitive 'said it all' simple sentence but labelling, ballooning, etc. Or they might start with a 'magnet' word in the middle of a piece of paper for other ideas to cluster around. This strategy is an excellent collaborative starting point for the teacher to scribe on blackboard, flip chart or OHP to which the whole class can contribute orally before embarking on private clusters of their own.

Young children can think in pictures inside their heads just as well as older children – and can transpose what they see behind closed eyes into words either orally or in their own writing. Children need to be shown how clever they are, all of them, as visualizers and as verbalizers because both capacities are powerful ways of shaping meaning. The teacher needs to share these mysteries about the workings of every human brain and create many opportunities for their constant use.

In their work in the late 1960s and early 1970s, on the development of writing abilities, the London Institute team under the direction of James Britton drew attention strongly to the issues of purpose and audience: 'Who for?' and 'What for?' Thanks largely to their work and to its incorporation in the Bullock Report these questions and the issues they raised led to another important shift in emphasis away from the teacher as sole audience and sole arbiter of all the writing that went on in schools to a search for more purposeful writing that would reach a wider range of readers. Writing and making real story books for real children is now commonplace and, in my experience, always successful. Computer programs such as Pendown and Front Page have boosted the motivation to present final products to a wider audience professionally and with pride. This is not to say that mindless, 'in a vacuum' writing has altogether disappeared; but it is not as prevalent as it was. My final point is more to do with an extension of writing purposes than a shift of emphasis. Most of the writing to which I have referred so far has been writing where the intention is to shape meaning into a finished piece – a 'product'. The different stages of development are designed to lead in that direction – from exploration to draft to revision to fair copy – the story of the poem or the article about bees or whatever.

But there is another kind of writing of great importance for learners which has steadily gained a foothold in some primary and secondary classrooms and which, ultimately, could be of more value to many children than the writing which turns into an artefact. I am referring to what is variously called think writing, log writing or journal writing. Such writing does not set out to become a product: its sole purpose is to help the writer to reflect. In this respect the most important audience is the writer herself as the writing is done in order to reveal to her thoughts and ideas that would not otherwise have gained any visibility at all. It helps a great deal, however, if the teacher is enthusiastic about the value of think writing and is willing to respond to pupils' journal entries uncritically but positively.

Journals, logs or think books can serve a variety of purposes. They can be used simply to encourage children to value their own thoughts and to have a book in which such thoughts can be caught before they vanish into thin air. For this purpose, particularly with young children, a class think book can be kept in which good ideas or intriguing questions are told to the teacher who writes them down so that they can be talked about and puzzled over at appropriate moments.

More directly related to the business of 'making sense' of a maths problem, of a science experiment or a poem – or indeed any new learning experience – is the fact that a pupil can use her think book to clarify what she is beginning to understand and to come up with questions for her teacher about some of her confusions. Pupils who have been encouraged to use their think books like this have appreciated the privacy of the dialogue that can be carried on with their teacher without others in the class overhearing.

Reading logs which fall into this 'making sense' category encourage readers to become more aware of the running commentary that sometimes takes place inside their heads when they are reading a book, and to write it down without the constraint of having to turn it into an essay. Some of the liveliest and most perceptive comments about novels, plays or poems that I have read over the past few years have come from pupils' reading logs. It is good to know that journal extracts (possibly chosen to reflect a reader's progress through a novel) can now be included as folder entries for GCSE.

Learning logs can both help the learning process along and reflect back over it. Teachers who invite children to take five minutes to work out why the liquid turned to green, or to jot down whatever has made the most immediate impact on them about the poem they have just read . . . are demonstrating that writing is a powerful way of thinking, especially if they keep and frequently write in their own log. Children have expressed surprise and astonishment that teachers actually bother to think about class activities. It does no harm to make such truths self-evident! It is quite possible to use think books for the exploratory phase of product-oriented writing. After all, all the brainstormed or clustered ideas might not be used in the draft once a focus has been found so it does no harm to save them for another time. Field notebooks and sketch books have been used by scientists and artists in much the same way. Writing and/or sketching in this way can be very useful as a pre-talking activity.

Then there is the looking back over what was accomplished in the lesson or possibly the week. Journals are not useful, in my opinion, for looking back over a longer stretch of time than that as the memory gets muzzy and tends to come up with broad generalizations instead of nitty-gritty details. In fact as far as individual profiling and self-assessment are concerned I believe that frequent log writing is essential if a termly or half-termly summary is to mean anything very much at all. Pupils can often work out for themselves how they can tackle a problem differently or plan what course of action to take next – but only if there is some immediacy to their decision making. In this way these two forms of reflection – mapping progress day to day and assessing over a longer period what progress has been made – are closely interlinked whether the teacher is the assessor or the pupil. One thing is for sure, no teacher however committed and conscientious can discover what 'sense' every pupil has been making of activities that have been jointly undertaken unless the pupils formulate those understandings (or confusions) for themselves. Journals, logs or think books provide both parties with an excellent way of telling.

As far as writing is concerned the last decade has produced all kinds of interesting developments for children of all ages and in many cases for teachers, too. The shifts of emphasis to which I have referred, will, I hope, become even more widespread as teachers share with colleagues the evidence of active learners writing to shape meaning with confidence and enthusiasm. There are all kinds of strategies still waiting to be developed that will help to sustain the efforts that genuine meaning making always demands in every area of the curriculum and at every phase of education. We have only just begun to find ways of convincing all children that they can become successful writers.

1   Making drafting work in the English classroom
SUE HACKMAN

Start your drafting experiments with a class whose confidence you have already secured. Do not expect them to know what to do: without your guidance they are likely to treat the first draft as a dress rehearsal and the second as a cosmetic finish. The best introduction you can give is to show them drafting in action. Get an overhead projector and show them how *you* do it. Pin up sequences of drafts on the display board, write when they write, and take them to the manuscript room of the British Museum to see the haphazard scribbles which evolved into the classic works of Wordsworth, Dickens and Austen.

Preliminary work might include mini-sagas (exactly fifty words of prose which must tell a story – no anecdotes or mere descriptions), visualization exercises and newspaper simulations which require synthesis and editing activities. Autobiography and 'snapshot' impressions are good starting points for more independent writing, but eventually pupils should take some responsibility for their own titles and audiences and for self-evaluation. Overzealous marking can take this sort of responsibility away from pupils and appropriate their work. Gradually allow pupils to take control of their own work in progress.

Do not take on the job of overseeing all the drafts yourself. You will not have the time, and the whole point of drafting is for pupils to take the initiative. Arrange the class into 'response groups' and establish guidelines for constructive criticism. Better still, get them to negotiate the guidelines. And do not feel guilty that you are not carrying the complete burden of response.

If pupils are working towards a specific end-product such as a piece of transactional writing for display make it easy for them by specifying from the outset the audience and purpose of the work and by making explicit any criteria by which you will assess the final piece. It is remarkable how often we keep our criteria secret.

Free pupils from anxious trifling by explaining that secretarial aspects such as handwriting, spelling and lay-out can be left to a late stage. This is a view endorsed by the national curriculum. Encourage commitment to this final stage by providing resources for good presentation and, above all, provide a real audience.

Be aware that drafting can be redundant. A precious personal experience can be diminished if it is treated as the occasion for writing practice. Drafts can also be time consuming and subject to the law of diminishing returns, especially for anxious pupils. Teach the art of letting go and do not let drafting become a drag. The biggest reservation I have about full prose drafts is that they can bring ideas into such high definition that fundamental changes are deterred. It is always worth considering alternatives such as telegrammatic notes, selected highlights, mental maps (e.g. star charts) and word processing.

Journals are harder to discuss because they take so many different forms – learning logs, creative writing notebooks, reading journals and so on. Because they ask of pupils a great deal of trust, journals should not be introduced in a peremptory way. If you have the time, introduce journals to individual pupils at a ripe moment. Always tell them why you think journals useful. For example, I always introduce reading journals to pupils with a simplified version of the talk I give to teachers about the 'active reader'.

Do not expect too much. Pupils take time to find a personal voice with which they feel comfortable. The idea of using writing to explore and experiment with ideas may well be new to them. Some pupils see journals as intrusive; respect their privacy, but create the optimum conditions for them to trust you. With some kinds of journal I have found it useful to publish a broadsheet of selected highlights. (Always ask first for the permission of contributors.) This usually stimulates a mood of experimentation and a period of vigorous journal writing. Setting out with a fixed model can inhibit the development of the individual voice, so it is best to offer plenty of models and support the emergent individual styles. Be ready for a wide range of entries, from idiosyncratic diagrams to highly disciplined prose.

There is ample opportunity within the curriculum for accurate considered retrospection: journals are a place to grasp fleeting ideas and develop them in writing. Pupils demonstrate in their journals how they think and learn. They are very personal. For this reason, journals should be confidential. It helps if you make positive, if discriminating, responses but desist from formal corrections which will deter spontaneity and confuse pupils about the status of the writing.

Journals work best in short bursts, between four to seven weeks. Longer than this and they become a ball and chain. I usually put journals on to an optional footing at around four weeks.

Drafts and journals are primarily for the pupil. The major benefits are derived at the time of writing, so they are useful self-help tools in the formative stages of learning. They belong to pupils, so treat them with respect and learn from the insights they give you into the learning process.

At the Creative Writing Course
Slightly frightened of the bullocks
as we walk into their mud towards them
she arms herself by naming them for me:
'Friesian, Aberdeen, Devon, South Devon . . .'
A mixed herd. I was nervous too,
but no longer. 'Devon, Friesian, Aberdeen . . .'
the light young voice chants at them
faster as the long heavy heads
lift and lurch towards us. And pause,
turn away to let us pass. I am learning
to show confidence before large cattle.
She is learning to be a poet.

(Fleur Adcock)

PART FIVE
Reading

5 A map of reading

NICK JONES

Sir, how do we know this is a poem? Well Charles, it is in a poetry book is it not? Poetry books are easily identified; the words poem or poet will appear somewhere on the jacket; inside, the print will not reach to the edge of the page. He is less sure of himself with those lines which will not reach to the edge of the page. He is less sure of himself with those lines that appear arbitrarily corralled amid the textual prairies of, say, the *Times Literary Supplement*. They seem to be poems because clearly they are not advertisements, but too often he finds himself wondering: why is this here? Why was it considered good enough to go in when possibly hundred of others more immediately accessible were not. Is it a GOOD poem? How do I know it is a good poem?

('Zeno was here' by Jan Mark)

Everything can be known about a reading public, back to the economics of printing and publishing and the effects of an educational system, but what is read by that public is the neutralised abstraction 'books', or at best its catalogued categories. Meanwhile, but elsewhere, everything can be known about the books, back to their authors, to traditions and influences, and to periods, but these are finished objects before they go out into the dimension where 'sociology' is thought to be relevant: the reading public, the history of publishing. It is this division, now ratified by confident disciplines, which a sociology of culture has to overcome and supersede, insisting on what is always a whole and connected social material process.

Raymond Williams (1977)[2]

I

This attempt to 'map' the process of reading arose in response to the question of *how we might interpret the notion of 'knowledge about language' in relation to the field of reading.* Both Kingman and Cox argued strongly for the encouragement of pleasure in reading, and for a significant breadth of reading experience. Both gave an especial weight, for secondary pupils, to the study of literature – 'the powerful and splendid history of the best that has been thought and said in our language' (Kingman, 2.22).[3] It was not in the remit of either committee, however, to establish the kind of framework for thinking about the reading process as a whole, which might help to answer that initial question. Nor, as a profession, do we possess for reading the kind of shared vocabulary of concepts and approaches which the national writing project has been able in its own field both to absorb and to generate.

The purpose of this chapter is therefore to offer for discussion a condensed but systematic account of reading/writing as a cultural practice. Because it attempts to mark out what is common to all reading its emphases will vary in relation to each particular instance. For the teacher the chapter maps ground to be considered both in the adoption of strategies for approaching individual texts, and in the context of broader, whole-school policies for reading development; these matters are the focus of the final section.

The map takes the form of a set of diagrams and a related commentary. The diagrams and the commentary together form an incremental sequence which looks in turn at different aspects of the reading process. Each section is keyed to a quotation from the Cox Report,[4] not in a spirit of biblical citation, but in order to locate the argument within the parameters of current legislation.

Diagrams are by their nature reductive – especially those conceived by other people. This very inadequacy, however, is a kind of invitation. Diagrams are perhaps most productive when they provoke in those who examine them a vigorous mental scribbling. By the same token the definitions which accompany the figures should be taken in the context of the argument about writers, texts and readings which the model itself proposes. These are the working definitions of a situated reader, frozen at the point of writing. Defrost at room temperature, and use your own recipes.

II

> Reading is much more than the decoding of black marks upon a page: it is a quest for meaning and one which requires the reader to be an active participant.
>
> (Cox, 16.2)

A common presumption of the relationship between writer, reader and text is that represented by Figure 5.1, in which the reader is seen as the passive receiver, or consumer, of the text which the writer produces. Or, by extension, the writer is seen as transmitting information – an instruction, an opinion, a report, a story – by encoding it within a text, from which a reader who shares that code (written standard English, for example) may subsequently retrieve it.

This individualized, oneway account does not, however, answer to the multiplicity and complexity of actual reading experience, and we might usefully extend and rework this model in a number of ways. To begin with, we need to comprehend the transactional or interanimative nature of reading relations: that what the reader brings to the text is as significant as what s/he takes from it. The arrows go both ways (Figure 5.1).

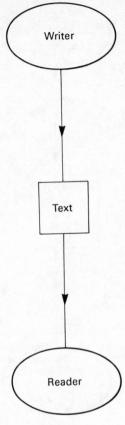

Figure 5.1

Second, we need to incorporate a sense of the differing *contexts* in which the act of writing and the act of reading separately occur (Figure 5.2).

III

> The full development of both reading and writing . . . requires a broad definition of text.
>
> (Cox 17.22)

Text

We can define a 'text' as any deliberate selection or combination of words, sounds or images in a stable form. While our major concern, as teachers of reading, is with printed verbal texts, the contemporary significance of video and other predominantly visual media, including illustrated books, means that these two

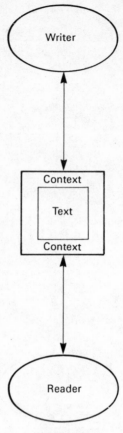

Figure 5.2

must come within our definition; spontaneous spoken language becomes a 'text' once it has been recorded and presented as such; at the boundary of our concerns we might regard clothing as 'textual' in a comparable way (cf. dress codes). For this reason you may prefer to replace the term 'writer' by a more general term such as 'composer'.

Texts are material objects, which carry within them the particular histories of their composition, and consequent possibilities of meaning. The term 'text' therefore implies both a reader and a writer. In its origin the word means something woven, which implies a purposeful working upon the available resources of meaning. The realization of this meaning, and the completion of the work, is none the less dependent upon the reader. It may be helpful to distinguish the 'text' – the material object – from the 'work' in this sense.

Reading texts does not, of course, exhaust the possibilities of reading. A meteorologist, for example, 'reads' natural signs; a detective 'reads' the accidental traces of human activity.

Context

All texts are read within a 'context' which conditions the reader's expectations and the interpretations which then appear possible; the context is indeed one part of the meaning that is communicated. The context will be different for different readers or for the same reader at different times. The reading context is to this extent beyond the control of the writer, who will none the less have written with certain ideal or possible contexts in mind. The marketing of books, as of other media products, is one of the more conspicuous and systematic aspects of this contextualizing process, and a reminder that there are intentions intermediate between those of writer and reader.

This double sense of the context of reading – the broad context assumed by the writer, and the particular context in which each reading occurs – is one aspect of its transactional or negotiated nature.

IV

Learning to read involves recognising that writing is made.

(Cox 16.13)

Composition

One part of the story of a text is the history of the choices made during its composition. A writer's intentions are always implicit within this process, whether or not they are overtly signalled within the text or deducible from it. It is impossible to read anything without making some assumption as to the writer's tone and purpose.

These intentions encompass the writer's sense (which may be no more than speculative) of the context in which the text will be received, including the envisaged readership, occasion, and purpose and the means of publication.

Somewhere in the writer's mind, though not always in the forefront, is the multiplicity of remembered models which makes it possible for writers to conceive of texts of this or of that kind. These might range from standard pro forma for simple writing tasks, to creative syntheses of otherwise quite disparate material. The various conventions for addressing or invoking an audience are one part of this discursive repertoire.

In the act of composition the writer works interactively upon the text as it emerges, often in the form of successive drafts (Figure 5.3). It is a common experience of writing that only through this process of trial and reflection does the writer gain a clear sense of what it is s/he is working to produce. The process of drafting therefore requires a constant shifting or oscillation of role from writer to reader; in the classroom or the workplace, that process may involve the active collaboration of other readers and other writers.

Each of these aspects of composition underlines the extent to which the

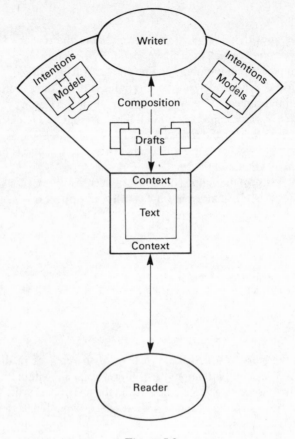

Figure 5.3

production of writing occurs within, and is dependent upon, a cradle of cultural relations.

V

> Children should know about the processes by which meanings are conveyed, and about the ways in which print and other media carry values.

> (Cox, 2.25)

Culture of production

The form a text takes during composition is dependent upon the means of the production of meaning available to this or that writer within a given culture. It is regulated by what is economically and technically feasible and by the relative degree of access to material resources. It is also dependent upon a writer's access to language, to the locked or unlocked storehouse of grammatical and rhetorical resources through which meanings are made. Both are aspects of the social history of that culture. Because language is always social, its forms and conventions are inscribed with the variable patterning of privilege or proscription, the ideological values which have been attached to certain modes of expression, or to certain categories of writing. Except in the most rigid of communities, these values do not go uncontested; new thoughts become thinkable as conventions emerge or recede. The definition of 'literature' is a recurrent example.

The writer

Within this culture of production, the writer occupies a position of tenuous independence. The alternative term, author, suggests a tradition of thinking that locates too simply the authority of the text, casting 'the' author as the solitary

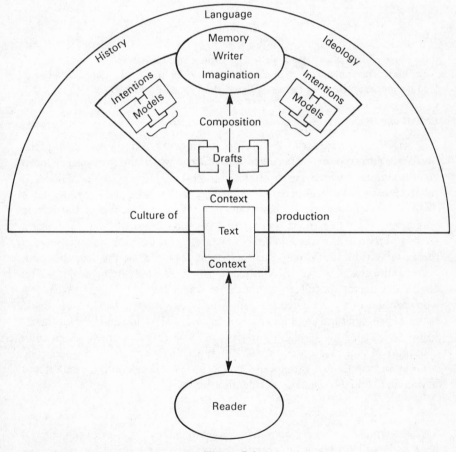

Figure 5.4

originator of meaning. Many texts are anonymous. Many are written by one hand but 'authorized' by another. Very often the writing process itself will be collaborative, as in most media products. What a writer does is not determined by culture but is always conditioned by it. At one end of the scale a writer may be employed by a particular set of commercial or political interests, or subjected to the constraints of a narrowly conceived assessment test. At the other, s/he may be writing a difficult love letter. The task is equally embedded in the available possibilities of the language. Figure 5.4 denotes the 'individuality' of the writer in three ways. Memory is the sedimented knowledge of our participation in a common history. Shifting and unreliable it none the less constitutes the uniqueness of the subject. Competence is one aspect of memory: that part of the repertoire of written forms and conventions that we have grasped and organized as our own. Imagination is the capacity of the human mind to think in metaphor, to fuse and to reconnect the elements of language and experience. It is imagination that renews and transforms the resources of a culture.

VI

Reading takes pupils beyond first-hand experience: it enables them to project themselves into unfamiliar environments, times and cultures . . . Reading is also one of the means by which we interact with the society in which we live.

(Cox 16.3/7)

Culture of reception

The sense which a reader makes of a given text depends upon the extent of the overlap or correspondence between the culture in which the text was produced and the culture in which it is encountered (Figure 5.5). It may be that writer and reader inhabit almost entirely the same 'cultural sphere', sharing the same dialect, the same history, the same values and conventions. Within the writing community of the classroom, for example, this will often be the case – though it would be an unusual classroom if this were always the case. At the same time, in the imaginary museum, or perhaps department store, of the late twentieth century, the reader/viewer is afforded an often dizzying choice of codes and allegiances. In such a culture the meanings which may attach to an object or a work are inevitably complicated; perceptions may range from a comfortable familiarity of signs and assumptions, to a sense of dislocation and bewilderment. Most difficult for the teacher, perhaps, are those cases in which an apparent continuity of language obscures real differences of usage or association. The historic and continuing promiscuity of the forms of English, both within and beyond the United Kingdom, is evidently a factor.

Reader

Like the writer, the reader both depends upon and can transcend the cultural patterns by which a text is underwritten. The social nature of codes ensures the possibility of meaning; the particularity of memory, the unique fusion of images and evaluations with which each reader accompanies the text, ensures its indeterminacy.

A reader's competence is not singular, and cannot be measured by a single indicator. It derives from all the uses of language that s/he has heard or read or practised. It will vary, for example, according to the reader's familiarity with the tokens of a particular genre, or to the degree of attentiveness which a text compels. Difficulty does not inhere in texts, but in the match between texts and readers; it is to that extent unpredictable.

In an important sense, the quality of a reading is unknowable outside the memory of the reader; it can be postulated only upon the basis of the talk or the writing that follows from it.

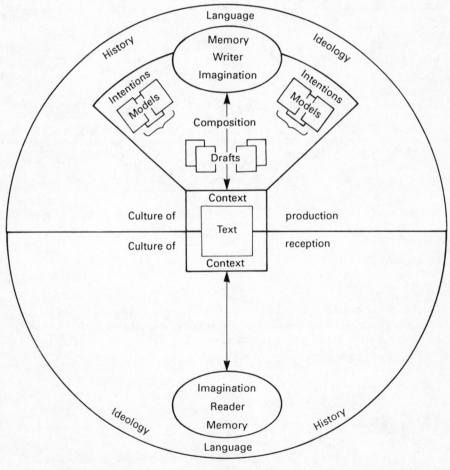

Figure 5.5

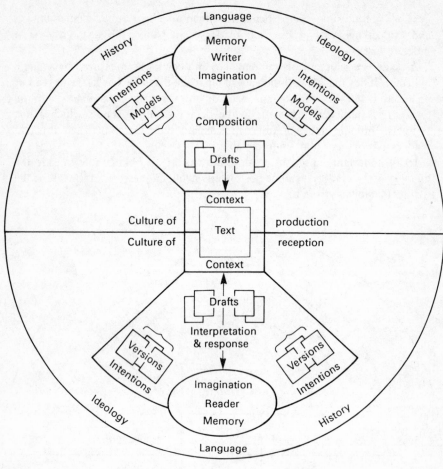

Figure 5.6

VII

The development of a methodology that is based upon informed concepts of reading and response rather than upon conventional, narrowly-conceived ideas of comprehension and criticism is now the priority.

(Cox, 7.22, quoting M. Benton)

Reading context

The process of reading, as here figured, is a reverse image of the process of writing: writing culminates in the text, and reading departs from it – or more accurately, from the text in its context.

The context of a reading, unlike that projected by the writer, is always localized and specific, and functions as a kind of frame, or coordinate. It tells the reader what to expect, what resources may need to be drawn upon. The reader's sense of context is therefore a mental construct and open to influence by the agencies of mediation. Expectations are shaped in ways which are both publicly and privately coded: by differences in editions; by differences in the mode of reproduction; by the various means through which a text can be recommended, prescribed or promoted; by associated brand loyalties or cultural aspirations.

Such perceptions are clearly bound up with the reader's own sense of his or her identity as a reader, particularly at the outset. Is this a book whose reader I wish to become? Is this advertisement/menu/parking ticket for the likes of me?

Textuality

The attentive reader inhabits the language of the text, examines the writer at work (or at play) within it. In this way, readers learn both to admire and to distrust writers; the reader who engages less closely with the machinery of the text is the less moved by it.

In their deployment of the rhetorical resources of language, texts direct the behaviour of readers in varying ways. The more 'open' a text, the more it encourages the play of memory or of intellect, and liberates or enlarges response. (This is one possible definition of 'literature'.) The more 'closed' a text – the workshop manual, the political interview – the more it aspires to close down interpretation and to coerce reaction. Closed texts require obedient readers. Good readers, however, decide when to submit to the authority of texts, and when to take liberties.

Interpretation and response

In Figure 5.6 the process of composition is mirrored by that of interpretation and response. This is one among many possible formulations: it is notable that there is a range of explanatory terms in educational use which point to aspects of reading (of which 'comprehension' and 'criticism', quoted above, are two of the commonest) and that its layered complexity is everywhere acknowledged.

The term interpretation insists upon the active nature of all reading. Readers make sense of texts only by drawing upon a knowledge which lies outside the text and by selecting, however provisionally, from among a range of possible inter-pretative frames and conventions. However habitual this process may sometimes seem it is never merely automatic.

At the same time the linking of interpretation with response is an acknowledge-ment that all readings are evaluative and ideological. What does this text mean, or not mean, to me? Does it give me pleasure? Does it earn my approval? The term response also points to the pragmatic force of reading, its power to prompt changes of thought or action.

This coupling of interpretation and response does not, however, imply successive operations: the one is always and already implicit within the other.

Interpretation might therefore be read in the musical sense: the 'score' of the text is realized in a performance – whether voiced or silent – which is both a decoding and a response.

Draft reading

Since reading is always a process of bringing meaning to a text, of collaborating with the text and its writer, it may be helpful to think of it in terms of the kind of 'drafting' with which we more readily associate the act of composition. First impressions may need correcting. The picture on the cover may turn out to have been a cheat. The reader's private forecasts as to the development of a plot or an argument may need to be adapted or abandoned. In schools this process of debate and refinement is often collective; but even the solitary reader experiences the dialogic nature of reading, matching and rematching the patterns of the language to his or her own knowledge of the world.

The development of this personal encyclopaedia of reference and probability will be especially marked over time and must be part of any notion of maturation in reading or in language understanding. The school rules that inhibit the intake year may be read differently by those with greater experience of the system in practice – as might the formula of a formula novel.

Modes of reading

Because this account seeks to represent the processes common to all reading, it has focused upon the multiplicity of texts, rather than upon the differences between them. The variousness of texts, however, invites a corresponding variety of modes of reading, and it is part of the process of interpretation and response to decide what kind of reading the text requires or deserves. Ought it to be read twice, for example? This is a matter both of insight and of disposition. Readers are offered positions by texts which they can accept or refuse. Readers too have intentions, and there may be many reasons for wanting to read against the grain of a text as the reader perceives it.

One commonly made distinction is that between reading for pleasure (or aesthetic reading) and reading for information. Though such distinctions are never absolute, the variability of intention is real enough and so is the range of appropriate reading strategies.

Similarly, aesthetic reading itself encompasses both the kind of reading which 'gets into' a book and travels with it, intent only upon arrival, and the kind which circles and contemplates until a meaning emerges. These differing responses are not purely a matter of text-type – the difference between a novel and a poem, for example. The same texts can be read in different ways and for different combinations of pleasure and information.

Versions: understanding

For all the above reasons, different readers come to different versions of the texts they consider, as may the same reader on a different occasion. In this way, readers develop their capacity for understanding. Understanding is not an activity, keyed to the reading of separate texts. It is a residue of feelings and insights which may be enriched or eroded by further reading and reflection. Fully to understand a text is to understand something of the culture in which it was produced or reproduced; how it comes to mean what it means; and who means it.

VIII

> As children read more, write more, discuss what they have read and move through the range of writing in English, they amass a store of images from half-remembered poems, of lines from plays, of phrases, rhythms and ideas. Such a reception of language allows the individual greater possibilities of production of language.
>
> (Cox 7.8, quoting Kingman, 2.23)

Intertextuality

The term 'intertext' is used to describe the associative networks of textual memory from which our sense of a culture is woven (Figure 5.7). It is not bound to particular cultures. Readers of print and of television across the world share many of the same stories, the same slogans, the same photographs. They need not, however, share the meanings they make of them. The intertext is not to be conceived as a body of material objects, as in a library. It is constituted only in the collective subjectivity of readers, in the fragmentary versions of texts which readers carry with them.

Each reader therefore constructs for her or himself this network of inter-relatedness. The nature of the observed connections will vary from generic resemblances between texts which may be commonly perceived, to chance personal associations. As individual memories are erased or overlaid the patterns to which they contributed may be weakened or may be reinforced by new readings.

The concept of the intertext encircles all the elements of this model. Much of what we know derives from it, in particular our literary competence. A reader's active sense of the forms and the conventions of language is derived less from formulated statements (such as this one) than from a complex diffusion of examples that suggest other examples. This draws attention to the double-sidedness of writing and reading: writers derive their models from the intertext, whether by unconscious influence or by conscious imitation; what they then construct is returned to it in the form of the textual versions which other readers fashion in response.

The concept of the intertext might be compared to that of literary tradition. The difference is that traditions are selective, and are defined or contested by the

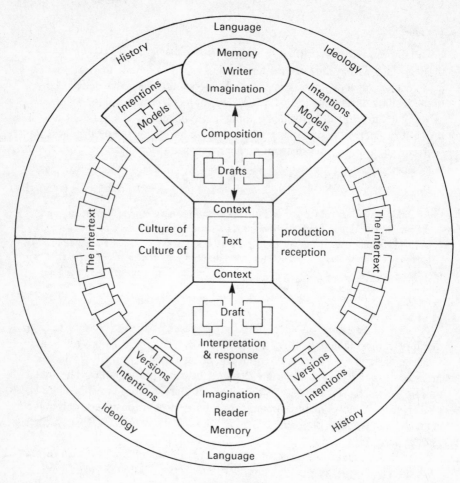

Figure 5.7

judgements of public bodies – publishing houses, reviewing panels, examination boards, universities. The intertext, on the other hand, is subjective and all embracing. Since it is constituted only in the memories of readers it cannot be institutionalized; it has no authority.

Meaning

The 'meaning' of a work is not to be found solely in the text itself, nor in the intentions of its producer, nor in the inventiveness of individual readers. Meanings are made in contexts, through the conjugation of readers and texts.

It follows that there are no single, authentic meanings – but nor is there an infinite possibility. The text is neither a transparent window nor a mirror. It focuses, blinkers, refracts, is sometimes opaque to, the eye of the reader.

Meanings also depend upon the vantage points of those who make them. They accrue and are scraped off, are haggled over and revalued. The poet's juvenilia are included in an appendix to the Collected Works; 'Instructions to servants' reappear on tea-towels in the gift shops of stately homes.

> In one sense, but a very limited sense, he [the writer] knows better what his poems 'mean' than anyone else; he may know the history of their composition, the material which has gone in and come out in an unrecognizable form, and he knows what he was trying to do and what he was meaning to mean. But what a poem means is as much what it means to others as what it means to the author; and indeed, in the course of time a poet may become merely a reader in respect to his own works, forgetting his original meaning, or without forgetting, merely changing.
>
> T. S. Eliot, *The Use of Poetry and the Use of Criticism* (1933)[5]

IX

No theoretical construct should be permitted to ride roughshod over what a school or department knows in its bones to be worth doing. At the same time there may be aspects of a school's practice which have turned ghostly, which have come to embody not inward conviction but a mere outward routine. The question then becomes, to what extent my reading of this text supports, or modifies, or brings into question, the way I think about reading as a whole.

The agenda which follows is purely speculative, to be drawn upon according to context and to need. The questions are loosely clustered, and assume a variety of overlapping perspectives. Taken together they invite a reconsideration of classroom practice in the light of the model proposed.

1 Questions of reading and writing – do children see themselves (and other children) as both writers and readers? Do these processes interlock? Do children know where books come from? Are there 'writers in school'?

2 Questions of fiction and non-fiction – is there a balance? Is there a boundary? Is it a subject boundary? Are fiction and non-fiction read in different ways? By different children? Is there also a balance between narrative and argument?

3 Questions of writing and literature – who defines literature, and according to whose values? Who chooses the texts? Is literature read only in English? How is it read? Do children see themselves as makers of literature?

4 Questions of identity and diversity – do all children get to read about themselves? About others? About themselves in the role of others? Are readers sometimes challenged or disturbed? Are cultural differences sometimes foregrounded? Is this a matter of texts, or of readings?

5 Questions of print and other media – how broad is the current definition of text? What are the priorities? How is the reading of images related to the reading of print? Is the idea of 'reading television' taken seriously?

6 Questions of context – if context is part of meaning, does it therefore need to be taught? Does this conflict with the principle of reading for pleasure? Does it call for an explicit consideration of cultural values and power relations?

7 Questions of style and rhetoric – do children come to perceive how the stylistic choices made by writers both constrain and enlarge meaning? Do they see a difference between argument and rhetoric? Do they learn how to unpick the threads of a text? Does this produce readers who are capable both of admiration and of distrust?

8 Questions of terminology – do children need a special language in which to talk about texts? About reading? How fruitful are the conventions of the book review? How does the established vocabulary of literary study compare with that of media study? Which terms are held in common? Which vocabulary is the more useful?

9 Questions of genre and intertext – do children encounter a wide range of text-types? How conscious are they of their own reading biographies, their own intertext? Do they make connections across media? Do they read one text in the light of another? Do they write in the light of their reading? Is there a place for direct imitation? For translation?

10 Questions of repertoire and process – do children discriminate between different kinds of reading, according to text and to purpose? Are they helped to do so? How are we to define 'advanced reading skills'? Are these skills transferable? Is 'information retrieval' a helpful notion? Are children able to take liberties with texts?

11 Questions of privacy and collaboration – what provision is made for solitary reading, and how does this relate to more participatory, collaborative forms of reading? How important is reading aloud, and to whom? Do children perform texts? In what ways are children encouraged to reflect upon the readings they have made?

12 Questions of interpretation and response – do children see their own responses as significant? The responses of other readers? Is there always scope for interpretation? For revaluation? For misreading? Do children consider the motivations of writers? With which broad categories of response are children most familiar? Do they work within, above, and beyond the text?

13 Questions of assessment – who determines the quality of a reading, and on what evidence? Are readers themselves the best judge of this? What criteria do readers use to judge texts? What criteria do they use to judge their own readings? How is such reflection encouraged?

A note on sources

This chapter has drawn loosely upon three broad areas of critical thinking. One is the tradition of aesthetic theory known as reader response, including particularly the work of Wolfgang Iser (*The Act of Reading* (Johns Hopkins University Press, 1978)), and Louise Rosenblatt (*The Reader, the Text, the Poem* (University of Southern Illinois Press, 1978)). The second is best represented by Raymond Williams's *Marxism and Literature* (Oxford University Press, 1977), for me the most coherent single study of the relationship of literature to ideology. The third influence is the semiotic tradition exemplified by the work of Roland Barthes (*Mythologies* (Paladin, 1972); *Image-Music-Text* (Fontana, 1977); *The Pleasure of the Text* (Hill and Wang, 1975)) and Umberto Eco (*The Role of the Reader* (Hutchinson, 1981)).

Other recommended reading

Margaret Meek, *How Texts Teach What Readers Learn*, Thimble Press, 1985.
Robert Scholes, *Semiotics and Interpretation*, Yale University, 1982, and *Textual Power*, Yale University, 1985.
Donald Fry, *Children Talk about Books: Seeing Themselves as Readers*, Open University Press, 1985.
Bill Corcoran and Emrys Evans, eds, *Readers, Texts, Teachers*, Open University Press, 1987.
Michael Benton *et al.*, *Young Readers Responding to Poems*, Routledge, 1988.

1   Reading autobiography
BRONWYN CADLE

As a part of sequence of INSET sessions which attempted to address some of the questions listed above one teacher produced a reading autobiography which she used subsequently as a focus for discussions about reading with her departmental colleagues. Many of her experiences have chimed with those of other teachers who have also started to reflect critically on their own classroom practice. See Figure 5.8 on page 98–9.

2   Nothing more than a story: a conversation with a teacher
JACK OUSBEY

In the corner of the classroom was a lifesize model of a young girl. She was wearing a long white dress with peppermint stripes of pink and green, a bathcap in matching colours, and ribbons and bows, also in pink and green. On her feet she had green slippers. She was holding, in both hands, a bunch of daisies, and alongside the model was a large card on which was printed:

> The dress had been perfect and so had the hat and so had the green slippers. She and the other girls all dressed the same, and the people had gasped with pleasure to see them in their peppermint stripes.

The card was edged with a pink and white floral pattern of daisies.

On the long wall of the classroom was an art gallery, part of which was given over to portraits. One of these depicted a very tall, long faced man with fair hair

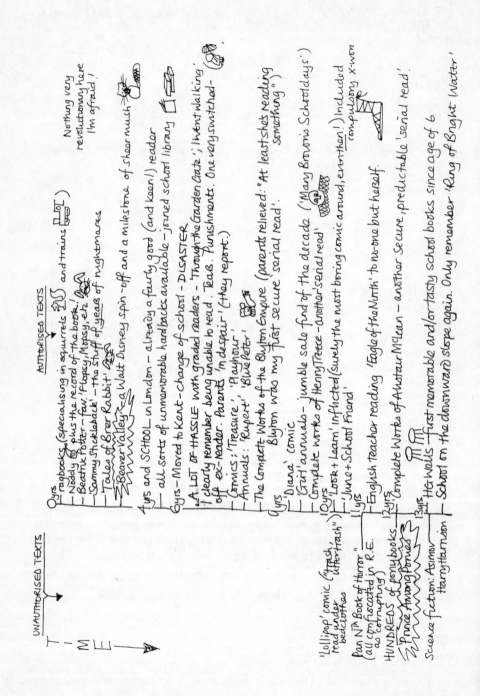

AUTHORISED TEXTS

0yrs — ragbooks (specialising in squirrels and trains)
- Noddy plus the record of the book!
- Beatrix Potter — fav: 'Flopsy, Mopsy' etc
- 'Sammy Shakleback' — the stuff of years of nightmares
- Tales of Brer Rabbit
- Beaver Valley — a Walt Disney spin-off and a milestone of sheer mush

4yrs and SCHOOL in London — already a fairly good (and keen!) reader
- all sorts of unmemorable hardbacks available — joined school library

6yrs — Moved to Kent — change of school — DISASTER
- A LOT of HASSLE with graded readers — Through the Garden Gate; I hate walking
I clearly remember being unable to read. Teas. Punishments. One very switched-
off ex-reader. Parents 'in despair' (Hay report.)
- Comics: 'Treasure', 'Playhour'
- Annuals: 'Rupert', 'Blue Peter'
- The Complete Works of the Blyton Empire (parents relieved: "At least she's reading something")
Blyton was my first secure 'serial read'.

8yrs
- 'Diana' comic
- 'Girl' annuals — jumble sale find of the decade ('Many Brownie School days')
- Complete works of Henry Treece — another 'serial read'

10yrs
- 'Look + Learn' inflicted (surely the most boring comic around, eventhan!) Included compulsory X-won
- 'June + School Friend'

11yrs
- English teacher reading 'Eagle of the North' to no-one but herself.

12yrs
- Complete Works of Alistair McLean — another secure, predictable 'serial read'.

13yrs
- HG Wells first memorable and/or tasty school books since age of 6
- School on the downward slope again. Only remember 'Ring of Bright Water'

UNAUTHORISED TEXTS

T
I
M
E

'Lollipop' comic ("trash, litter-trash") read under bedclothes

Pan Nth Book of Horror" (all confiscated in R.E. as corrupting)

HUNDREDS of pony books — 'Prince Among Ponies'

Science fiction: Asimov, Harry Harrison

Nothing very revolutionary here I'm afraid!

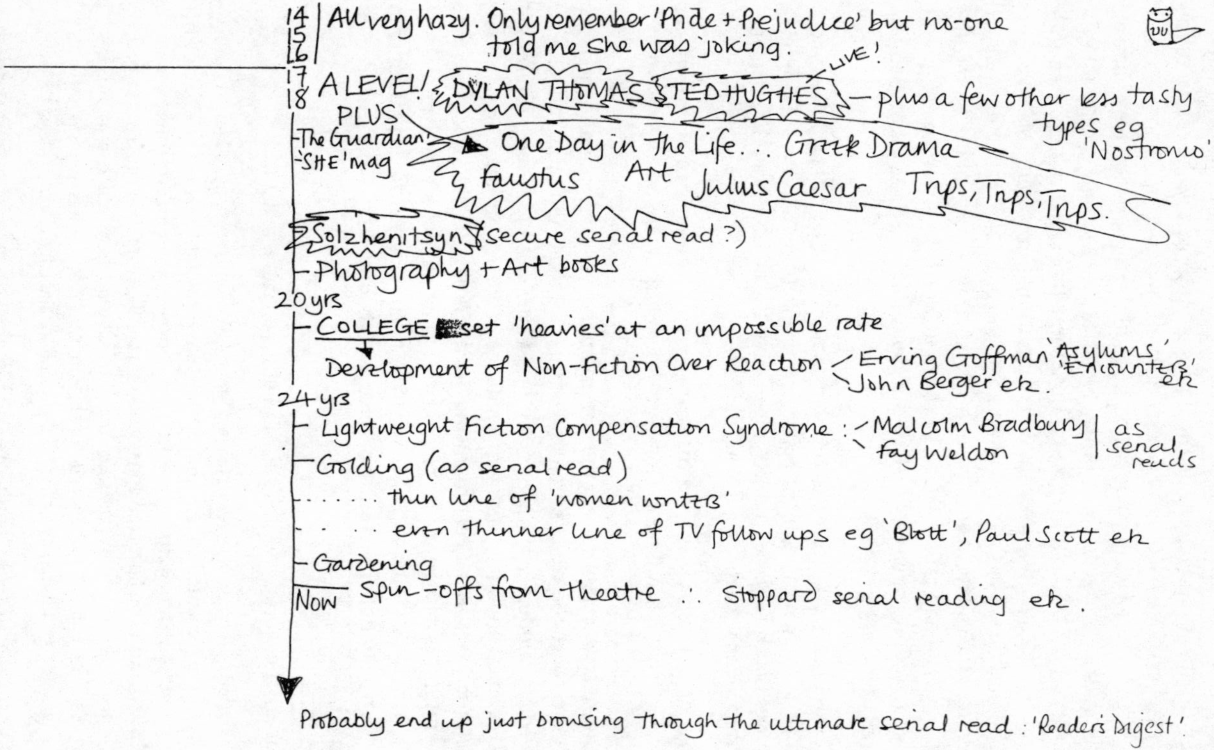

[DW]

14 | All very hazy. Only remember 'Pride + Prejudice' but no-one told me she was joking.

15 |
16 |
17 | A LEVEL: DYLAN THOMAS, TED HUGHES — plus a few other less tashy types eg 'Nostromo'
"we!"

18 PLUS
The Guardian → One Day in the Life ... Greek Drama
'She' mag   Art   Julius Caesar   Trips, Trips, Trips.
        Faustus
Solzhenitsyn (secure serial read ?)
– Photography + Art books

20 yrs
– COLLEGE set 'heavies' at an impossible rate
Development of Non-fiction Over Reaction < Erving Goffman 'Asylums'
                                            John Berger eh. 'Encounter' eh

24 yrs
– Lightweight Fiction Compensation Syndrome :- Malcolm Bradbury
Golding (as serial read)   Fay Weldon | a.s. serial reads
.... thin line of 'women writers'
..... even thinner line of TV follow ups eg 'Blott', Paul Scott eh
– Gardening
Now Spin-offs from theatre :. Stoppard serial reading eh.

Probably end up just browsing through the ultimate serial read :'Reader's Digest'

Figure 5.8   Reading autobiography

and gold rimmed glasses, dressed in a pale grey suit and a purple waistcoat, labelled Lonesome Jones. Alongside him was Rosie, the rosiest bride imaginable, in a dress as pink as the brightest pink you ever saw. There were pictures too, of the wedding ceremony itself, and views of London at night-time with dark domes and spires, and boats and barges on the Thames. And right in the centre of this display was a beautifully decorated, larger than life, wedding invitation.

On another wall a series of coloured photographs had been mounted, showing the wedding itself. There was the bride, Rosie, and her father, getting into the wedding car; there was the bridegroom, Lonesome Jones, waiting at the church; there were the bridesmaids with a number of guests at the reception. Each picture had a text alongside it advising the viewer about the proceedings. A huge painted map hung from the ceiling at one end of the room. It was a map of England with a single link, by road and rail, between Leyburn in North Yorkshire and London. Alongside each of these places, illustrated accounts of people and events were set inside large frames.

> 'This is the farm at Bank Heads Pasture', the Leyburn one began, 'where Lonesome Jones took his caravan on a painting holiday and first met Kit. And here are three of the pictures Lonesome Jones painted at the farm. He paid his rent to Kit's dad by giving them original paintings of Kit and the farm.'

And alongside the railway line, on the map, were a number of thought-bubbles which showed what Kit and her father were thinking as the train headed south for London.

There were book exhibitions in the classroom too. (I nearly called them home made but they were too well crafted and written for that.) One was called, *Kit's First Exhibition*, another, *Kit's Diary*, another, *Crisis at Bank Heads Pasture*. Yet another contained bound copies of an exchange of correspondence between Kit and Lonesome Jones in the year following the wedding.

By now my interest had gone far beyond the casual: something exceptional was happening in this classroom and I needed to know about it. I invited the teacher to meet me to chat about her literature project, and about the displays I had seen on my extended visit.

Tell me about the work I saw will you, and how you came to set it up?

> Jane Gardam is a favourite writer of mine.[6] She has written a story called *Kit in Boots*, which I liked and wanted to use with my eleven-year-olds. It is about a famous painter called Lonesome Jones who goes each year to paint in the Yorkshire Dales. He parks his caravan on farmland and comes into conflict with the farmer, Kit's dad, who is a pretty dour sort of Yorkshire man and doesn't have much time for arty southerners. The tale shows how relationships develop, and it has a young girl as a central character which makes a change. I wanted to share it with my class.

But English teachers don't usually operate like this, do they, with paint and glue and displays of work, and with children actually making and illustrating their own stories? Do you work like this all the time?

Whenever possible. GCSE coursework has opened up the way to a much more creative style of working. In any case there are no impediments to using such approaches in years 1–3. I reckon I tackle two or three books a term in this way. You see, some books seem to invite this kind of treatment. As you read them you can sense all the possibilities, all the exciting developments you might share with children.

But doesn't it leave you wide open to criticism? Why are you spending so much time on one book? Why are you getting children to paint and act and make models, when it is your job to teach them how to use language in a competent way?

I have no difficulty in answering questions like that, as long as I am given time to explain the reasons why I work in this way. In the first place it is about the way children learn anything. If you watch a child at work and observe closely what they do, it soon becomes clear that they like to be involved, they want to participate and help to take control of the activities. I have also noticed that they seem to respond better if they can set their own rules and find out for themselves how they would like to operate. When they are working at their best, they aren't conscious of things like 'learning' or 'skills' or 'development', they just enjoy exercising their talents. A book like *Kit in Boots* allows the teacher to operate in that way. And I am not spending all that much time on one book, when you consider that language and literature are being taught together here. When children are using language in such a creative way, with a real sense of self imposed purpose, they don't need rule-governed materials as well. Their interest in editing and reshaping means that they are seeking all the time to improve the technical side of the work. We have an editorial advisory group, picked by the children, which changes each week, to comment and advise on work for publication. And another thing I have discovered is that many creative activities are much more successful if people work together in pairs or small groups.

You're not suggesting, are you, that children don't learn when they work quietly and individually, on an assignment set by the teacher and directed by her?

Not at all. Learning occurs almost all the time, in the most unlikely and difficult situations, as well as in the most favourable. My observations and practice tell me – convince me – that useful, lasting learning is more likely to happen when children are cooperating, are happy, and have a say in what is going on. It is commonsense, and it works.

Right, I'll agree to that. But tell me about the diversions – painting, photography, dressing up, mask making, models and so on?

You are assuming, without hesitation, that these activities are diversions, just frills or some kind of optional extras. They are not. They are powerfully bound up with language development and with understanding. Let's take painting a portrait as an example. The child listens to the teacher read the story, and, whilst doing so, processes the events, descriptions and ideas 'inside the head'. There is a lot of evidence to show what goes on when a reader, or a listener, activates a story. Mental pictures of people and places are created. We build up a portrait of, say, Lonesome Jones by listening to the physical descriptions of him in the story and by finding out what he does, how he responds and reacts, and what sort of man he is. We also bring to the story our individual experiences and views of people who are painters and from this kaleidoscope we build up an image of the man Lonesome Jones. Transposing all these things – the text, the images, the preconceptions – into a painting is a thinking activity as well as a physical one. We use words and ideas, almost always sub-vocally, to consider, adjust, reflect upon, recall and arrange all the impressions we have encountered in order to change them into a painting. Transposing from one form to another, from one medium to another, is an activity which draws on the language stores we have in our heads.

Furthermore, my children are invited to talk to each other whilst at work. Often they will explain what they are doing to another child or to me. Sometimes they will be asked to do this in front of a group or the whole class. We ask each other questions about the size of the portrait, or the way the colours are mixed, or the different textures which can be obtained in the mixing of the paint. Children learn language by encountering and using it; by feeling comfortable in an environment where talk is required and expected; by learning to expand and explain their ideas; by being challenged to use words precisely and imaginatively. Painting a picture in this way is worth more than all the exercises in English course books.

I suppose it is. And I presume you have a similar defence for the other activities – the dramatic recreation of the wedding, the lifesize models, and so on?

The quality of the work and the children's interest speak for themselves. It is the people who practise a 'systems and structures' approach who should be called upon to defend what they do. It is the spurious, the phoney, the mechanical, the trivial practices we need to attack. Just consider the map the children constructed and what that entailed. The decision to make a map was one they came up with – a small group, that is. They wanted to show the difference between the isolated, farming family in North Yorkshire and the art world of London. They also wanted to link them up through the wedding. Their discussion about how they could do this arose from a corporate sense of excitement about the possibilities. They were full of ideas – extravagant, amusing, sometimes absurd – about the project, and used language to explore and consider, to challenge and reject, to decide on what should be done and how the work should be divided up. And in the construction of the map itself they were involved in labelling, describing, listing and writing dialogue, as well as in animated discussions about the mechanics of actually making it. All those factors I mentioned earlier, about young children and learning, figured in the map-making work.

But amid all the bustle of group work and the creative activities, isn't it possible that the story disappears, gets submerged? Wouldn't it have been better just to have read and enjoyed it together?

We did read it together and enjoy it. That's how it began. And with some books that might be all we want to do. But, in this case, we've all got inside the story. We have inhabited Kit's world and the world of Lonesome Jones. We feel that we know them as people, and even though they are only characters in a story, they are now fairly close acquaintances of ours. We understand their attitudes and their likes and dislikes. And in return for engaging us in their world, in the secondary world of story, we have invited them, now, into the primary world of our school. For a short time we have adopted them. And we have tried to find out what it might be like to be an angry, suspicious farmer, or a young girl from the Dales on her first visit to London. I reckon that Jane Gardam's story has helped some of us to grow a bit, as well as providing us with a rich resource for language work.

You would go as far as that, would you? Stories help children to 'grow a bit', to understand other people's viewpoints. It's a bit of a sweeping claim, isn't it?

Not at all. Stories have always done that, for as long as language has been available to us. The development of the world's great religions has depended on stories; the tragedy and ecstasy of human experiences are revealed to us through story; story brings us face to face with alternative possibilities in a way which is both accessible and compelling. We can't do without stories. They permeate our waking and sleeping worlds. No, I have no doubt about what stories can do. They are not just sources of great verbal energy. Stories can do things for us, and to us, providing they are good stories, stories which have endured or are going to endure.

Oh, I see. There's a qualification is there? They have to be 'good' stories, whatever that means?

Absolutely. As teachers we are charged with by society to educate the children in our care. That means we are responsible for providing the best we can in the way of experiences, materials, activities, and particularly in terms of literature. We can't escape that duty. You wouldn't want your own children spending time with stuff that was third rate, would you?

But 'good' is a relative term. Who decides what is good when you're going to use books in your classroom?

We do. We try to, anyway. It is another one of those responsibilities we cannot shirk. As a department we read and discuss, reject and then select the stories we will use with our classes. We are a 'reading department' and we have to have a set of standards by which we judge the books we read. How else could we operate?

Maybe you are right. But what do these criteria look like?

They are not final, once-and-for-all measures, though some of them remain pretty constant. We look for stories which are written with a language which is sociable – that is, it draws the reader into the tale sometimes quite effortlessly, like Alan Garner's *Stone Book* quartet. There's a friendly text, if ever there was one. It simply invites the reader to enter into its community. It's a most comfortable, welcoming set of books. We reckon that a good story will have a truthfulness about it, too, which is apparent and appropriate. Notice, I talk about truthfulness not reality. There is a difference. If you have read Susan Cooper's '*The Dark is Rising*' sequence, you will know what I mean. The world Susan Cooper describes in those tales does not match with the objective, scientific, neutral, so-called world of reality, but it does, nevertheless, deal with things which are important and true. And, incidentally, fantasy itself is a powerful kind of reality. Susan Cooper's stories leave us feeling that the only possible way to tell the tale was in that particular way, using that language and no other. If you tried to tell it or read it using a different language, it would cease to be that story.

We also feel that good stories give space to the reader or listener, to make contributions. They don't try to deal with every minute detail; they don't tell you how to react or think; they credit you, the reader, with an imaginative faculty which they wish to engage. Helen Cresswell's stories do these things superbly well. If you've read *The Outlanders* or *Winter of the Birds*, or two of her latest stories, *The Secret World of Polly Flint* and *Moondial*, then you will know what I am talking about. And I must say, as a department, we like stories that puzzle and challenge as well as reveal. Jannie Howker is a writer who can do that. She has a passion for people and places which can be a bit disturbing. Both *The Nature of the Beast* and *Isaac Campion* are stories about extremes. They show how children have to rely, sometimes, on their outlaw selves to generate the spirit and energy to cope with an unfair world.

Then again, we hope that a good story would have its own rhythm and movement, its own variations in pace and emphasis, that it will 'step out' in a way which compels the reader to pick up the tune and join in the march. Have a look at the beginning of James Thurber's marvellous tale, *The Wonderful O*, or try reading out loud the opening of *The Iron Man*. You can't help but be impressed by the song and dance of the words in those two stories. Above all, we look for tales which take the reader inside the story world so that, for a short time, they stop being part of this world and enter the one created for them by the writer.

Anything else?

Well, not all of us agree, every time, about every book. Our selections are coloured by our own experience. But we do try to use high quality stories when we share a book with children. It's not censorship. We don't prevent children choosing from class and school libraries whatever authors or titles they like. We do think that teaching time is limited, however, and the two hundred minutes or so we get each week for our English classes should be filled with the best, however short we may fall in defining that category. Children shouldn't get through school without encountering writers like Philippa Pearce, Leon Garfield, Rachel Anderson, Julian Atterton, Betsy Byars, Nina Bawden, Paula Fox – I could go on. And we have a strong commitment to keeping the very best picture books in front of our classes. Raymond Briggs and Michael Foreman, Rodney Campbell and Mitsumasa Anno, Maurice Sendak and Russell Hoban. Especially Russell Hoban.

At some time during their school lives all children should read Hoban's *How Tom Beat Captain Najork and his Hired Sportsmen*. It's a tale that deals with the endless possibilities of the creative imagination, and represents, to children, the anarchic world of which they are a part.

Is it possible to look at the kind of preparation you undertake when you work on books like the ones you have mentioned?

I prepare a set of working notes. At my first reading of the book I jot down all the possible ways of developing the story I can think of, plus any ideas I might have for organising the groups and the activities. Usually I start by writing down bits of the text which might interest a child, or a group of children. And alongside these references I note down possible ways of working, but I would want the children to take up the text themselves, to examine it and make their own suggestions. Then, after a second reading, I produce a bank of possible assignments from which children can choose if they wish. What I am trying to do is to set a kind of boundary for the work within which the children can negotiate and choose their own work. I want to create a 'holding form' that offers a rich source of ideas and possibilities. Here it is. You can read it for yourself.

Working notes for *Kit in Boots* by Jane Gardam

Part of the text which might be developed:

Kit looked at the dress hanging there, and the soft pretty hat and particularly at the green slippers every night as she fell asleep.	Owning things; wanting to own things; looking at things in shop windows.
Also, Kit's father, the farmer, would have roared like his own terrible bull and eaten for breakfast anybody who dared to park a car on his land.	People, as animals or birds; "The Furniture Game" compiling a list.
'Good smell,' said the man. 'Paint is my petrol. Smell of life.'	Smell-associations with occupations; collection of sayings.
'Work – rubbish,' said her father, enjoying himself. 'Good to be some folk muscle work's what counts.'	Earning one's living: work or play? footballer; painter; miner; window-cleaner, etc.
'Can you imagine my father in London?'	Imagining parents, relatives, in unlikely places; collection of 'Imagine my . . .' sayings.
A paper fluttered out from the envelope, too, and Kit's mother picked it up.	Predicting; writing the letter in the style of Lonesome Jones.
'My father says you're Lonesome Jones.' He liked that and smiled to himself.	Nicknames – work in a group; consult parents/grandparents to compile list of nicknames.
'It's to be in London. Great Guns – think of the train fares. They're the price of a heifer.'	Two fares to London; equivalent to . . . . if you were a . . . .
Kit who had already written to Lonesome Jones accepting the invitation, wrote again (with illustrations) to bring him up to date with all the latest arrangements.	Letters and illustrations; a letter, written but never sent, from Kit's Dad to Lonesome Jones.
They stood in the London station with the cheese and the suitcase, and people whirled and ran about and butted and shoved them.	Strange environments; crowded places; stations; shopping.

And Kit longed and longed for tomorrow to come. Which, of course, it did as tomorrow does and then it was over as tomorrow is.

Expectation; excitement and waiting; The Great Day.

'Thank you for being such a good bridesmaid and for bringing in your father. He's a famous man, you know. His face is going to live forever.'

Living forever – in paint – other ways; how would you like to live forever?

Possible titles for paintings

Kit in boots; Kit in stripes; Kit's mum and dad; the baby Lisa; the farm days; the Muscovy duck; the terrible bull; the three velvet apple trees; the farmhouse with the wind round it; the train journey; the railway station; the church; the wedding; the reception; London at night.

Possible written assignments

Wedding invitations; wedding menus; Kit's dad's school report signed by Miss Bell; Lonesome's letter to Kit inviting her to be a bridesmaid; Dad's letter (never sent) explaining why they couldn't go to London; exchange of letters between Kit and Lonesome after the wedding; Kit's diary from meeting Lonesome to the day of the wedding; Miss Bell's letter to her London relatives.

Labels and texts to go along with the displays.
Lists for packing to go away; for wedding presents.
Captions for photographs.
Stories using all the characters encountered in the story, e.g. Kit's First Exhibition; Lonesome Jones Helps Out; Miss Bell's Retirement Party.

Drama work

The family debate the invitation to London.
A re-creation of the wedding – with guests? photographer? reception?

Story telling

Re-telling the story as a group presentation, each group having an audience from another class.

Other work

Models – lifesize? Photograph album or display of photographs. A map or plan of the farm, based on the text.

Working notes

1 Read the story through at one go, purely for enjoyment.
2 Discuss possibilities with class, listing on a planning chart all their ideas, to which they can add.
3 Discuss ways in which we can work – individually, in pairs or small groups – and make decisions about procedures.
4 Decide how many copies of the book we shall need (6?) for reference.
5 Possible second reading with children listening, not following the story in their own copies.

What do I want the children to do during the project?

Listen; discuss; read; question; suggest; cooperate; write letters, labels, diary entries and stories; paint; model; make plans and diagrams; play roles; re-create; re-tell; transpose and compose.

Conclusion

Invite another class in to visit and view?
Suggest a presentation to parents?
Re-enact 'wedding' for assembly?
Do it just for fun?

3   Teaching the long novel –
Our Mutual Friend
PAM BARNARD

The Penguin edition of Dickens's *Our Mutual Friend*,[7] with Stephen Gill's introduction and notes, has over 900 pages; it weighs one pound. Handing it out to 18 students in the late summer of their first year of 'A' level study produces an immediate range of responses, from gentle resigned sighs to expostulations of disbelief.

So that's where we start. What does the size of the book tell us about the readership for whom this novel was first written? What scale of concerns might the author have? What potential and problems in plotting? The resulting speculations are to be tested later against the experiences of the first headlong read. This introduction finishes with some biographical and cultural snippets of information of a scandalous and entrepreneurial kind about serialization and Dickens's working methods.

A second session focuses on titles (of the novel itself, its four volumes and the chapters); what does *Our Mutual Friend* suggest to you? I have been staggered by how students respond to the suggestiveness of the three words. They pick up the core of mystery; the novelist trying to intrigue his readers and invite them into the text; the promise of delayed revelations. The ambivalent nature of friendship in the novel is sensed and explored. Why *our* friend, not *yours*? Students pursue the suggestion of an inner, almost 'old boy' network – which they later see Dickens exploiting in Podsnap's and Veneering's prosperous middle-class snobbery, and in the poignant comic dimension of Twemlow's miniature traumas. There are responses to the legalistic delicacy of 'mutual' and ideas that someone – lawyers perhaps – cannot be open about who is actually 'our mutual friend'. Then, if speculation runs on long enough, someone hits on the idea of a conspiracy between the writer and the reader; after all, he or she is *our* mutual friend.

Moving through the four titles to the books which made up the novel, the students rumble the proverbial dimensions with their implications of groups of characters mistakenly thinking that they're in control; 'There's many a slip 'twixt cup and lip', the dismissive 'Birds of a feather' and the notion that 'It's a *long lane* which has no/*a turning*' which says something about sustained and difficult courses of action finally producing positive results and a deserved conclusion.

To read a narrative so sustained and diverse for a final examination question needs readers who are intrigued by such overarching patterns and authorial purposes. So 'teaching the long novel' in an 'A' level course is about finding ways into a reading which will confirm students' confidence that they can handle such length; that their responses, initially in the form of hunches and expectations, are perceptive; and, fundamentally, that such a large novel positively encourages multiple readings.

The summer vacation is for their first reading supported by a little red book, written by a colleague. Focusing on plot and character it introduces each chapter with a brief question or comment, then invites the reader, in true serial fashion, to 'read on'. The guide then confirms a reading with a brief plot summary and invites prediction, recapitulation or speculation.

Having encouraged students to reflect the original serialized form of the book in the way they carry out their own first reading, I spend the last session before the vacation on the opening chapter. After as dramatic a reading aloud as I can manage, I ask them in pairs to produce a series of rapidly sketched and annotated 'stills' for the opening sequence of their film of *Our Mutual Friend*. A comparison of these versions reveals shared and diverse readings. It also alerts them to Dickens's techniques of visual presentation; and when they discuss what they *cannot* present filmically, they begin to recognize those aspects of tone, sub-text and authorial comment which a predominantly visual medium rarely encompasses ('but Gaffer was no neophyte and had no fancies').

The autumn term of the second year begins with what to an outsider preoccupied with the rigours of study might see as a 'gush session', but its aim is to look at Dickens's appeal to a variety of readers and how, in all his modes of writing, comic, satiric, straight narrative and rhetorical, his themes and concerns emerge. Students group themselves according to 'favourite episodes' and prepare a presentational reading. The Veneerings' dinner party and the introduction of the Wilfers are frequent choices, together with 'Wegg's leg' and Jenny Wren's 'come up and be dead'.

Groups then draw a vast pyramid, a 'dust-heap' to represent the society of the novel. Characters are placed first on that dust-heap according to social status, provoking discussion on 'who parasites on whom'. Images or connecting lines suggesting the recycling of rubbish. The movement of money and its substitutes of shares, bills and wills can be labelled. The students then place the same characters on the pyramid again according to moral worth. The result is not a thing of beauty (an overlaid OHP sheet would have been a better strategy) but the resulting discussion is energetic. Lizzie's movement through the dust-heap, Podsnap's unassailable position at the financial peak and his relegation to the moral base, the sheer numbers of those recyclers of waste are sharply exposed, from Jenny Wren fabricating dolls of fashion from her bits and pieces to Benus's articulated skeletons.

With such a vast novel students need to feel secure in some area of expertise. They require knowledge of an aspect of the text which will enable them to discuss with confidence such abstract notions as 'money, politics or power', a multiple plot and at least four distinct styles of writing. A way into this expertise is for each of them to create a character chart on someone in the novel who interests them. If they choose a major character, such as Lizzie, they can pair up because of the volume of event and reference; if it's a single-faceted minor character such as Sloppy, they double up on another character allied in the plot, such as Mrs Boffin. They then have a week to prepare character charts on A3 plain paper with an androgynous figure in one corner to dress and label with characteristic gestures and speech bubbles, such as Mrs Wilfer's knotted handkerchief, Podsnap's dismissive wave or Jenny Wren's 'I know their ways . . .'.

The discovery that more rounded characters lose such signatures early in the novel, as with 'gloomy Eugene', sharpens discussion on characterization. The accompanying debate around the literary terms of 'grotesques' and 'caricatures' is inevitably fierce, for their readerly perceptions differ about who is credible or exaggerated, predictable or static. As for presentation of the young women in the novel, battle lines are drawn early. Bella is 'sickening', 'manipulative', 'wet' and Lizzie is 'too good to be true'. Others stand further back and argue from socio-political positions. Despite protocols of textual evidence and an openness to other readings consensus is never reached, but early emotive utterances have, I think, been tested and tempered by probing questions and more measured argument.

Thematic concerns such as the Poor Law and education; romantic love and the family; class division and legal and financial practices are specialized in by small self-selected groups. Supplementary non-fiction evidence may come from Mayhew's *London Labour and the London Poor*,[8] Horne's *Household Words*, extracts from social histories; and I build up a wall display, without much comment, of what seem to be relevant articles from current newspapers showing, I hope, that the issues are still live and unresolved. Group presentations with

OHP, posters and readings summarize their studies and the listeners try to make connections with their own topics. The process is not about becoming expert on every 'theme' but to see, firstly, how a system of values operates through each theme, to question those values and, secondly, to see how a literary term such as 'theme' is a way of framing a response and is not a 'fact' within a text.

One month's study of this text does not allow relentless chapter by chapter close reading. But in order to keep the language of the novel constantly in mind, we share regular rehearsed readings and a detailed study of a substantial section of a chapter. In this way, my hope is that students will both relish the detail of the text and yet expand their overview of the landscape of the novel as a whole.

4 Teaching fiction 5–11
DOT FROGGATT

In the same way that children long to have adventures, I believe books cry out to be explored and I often use fiction as a starting point for rich, cross-curricular projects. As soon as I sense a class has become hooked on a book I am reading to them, I take the children on a journey deep into the story or bring parts of it out to be lived in the classroom. In this way I can combine using the endless source of literature with the imagination of the class, to provide exciting experiences in which the children are directly involved.

I have worked in this way across the primary phase from reception infants to top juniors, using picture books, poetry, simple text, contemporary and traditional children's fiction, as well as extracts from adult literature. The highly acclaimed *Nicobobinus*,[9] by Terry Jones, has been an ideal book in which to involve children.

Nicobobinus and his friend Rosie had last been heard of by the class sailing away on a mysterious ship and in great danger. The children were working on maps of their journey so far and trying to predict the route, when a large brown-paper parcel was delivered to the class. Curiously they opened it and found a heavy, ornately carved piece of wood with a label tied to it that said simply, 'Please help! Nicobobinus'. I denied any knowledge of the parcel and the children became involved in fierce debates and frenzied investigations as they tried to solve the mystery of the parcel and its connection with Nicobobinus. They re-read the story searching for clues and turned to atlases and reference books on history, Venice, shipping and explorers for further information. They decided that the carved wood was a piece of the ship upon which Nicobobinus was sailing and that something awful had obviously happened. I continued reading the book to them and at this point, the children were now a part of it and deeply involved. Poetry, additional chapters, biographies of the characters, letters of enquiry, reviews, analyses and summaries were all written as the story gradually unfolded. Mathematical, scientific and design problems all based on the book were discovered, challenged and solved as models, drawings, puppets and sculptures were being created. Gold and its formation was an important part of the story and the children were soon involved in a parallel adventure of their own as they attempted to make it. Trying to produce a gold pigment that satisfied their requirements (neither yellow nor orange) proved to be an enormous challenge that sent them to artists, buildings, myths and legends. Their own discovery that green was required was cause for much satisfaction and generated widespread interest as they reported their find to others.

By now, Nicobobinus and Rosie were so real that the children were tackling complex issues in order to identify and locate their time and place of existence. Terry Jones had set the story 'a long time ago' but the children felt they knew more about the characters than their creator and concluded they were in a circle of time that embodied the past, present and future. They supported their theories with evidence from the book; discoveries made during their own adventures and knowledge acquired as a result of their investigations and enquiries. For example, gender dominance and stereotyping by the media, including literature, were discussed avidly and they placed the book's central characters into the present or future, otherwise how could Rosie have played such an active, dominant role? The children were firmly convinced that she was not of the traditional folktale genre. A growing sense of history and historical evidence bugged the children back to the past, while further adventures in the book triggered off new experiences in the class and the present. Amazing really that Terry Jones managed to write the book without them! But it was as if he knew that children had to become directly involved in his book and participate in the ending. He provided an eminently satisfactory outcome for his story of Nicobobinus, yet at the same time left such an open ending that the children were able to weave in their experiences and I was able to continue and develop them, thus perpetuating their reality of Nicobobinus, bounded only by the limits of their imagination.

Combining the characters and incidents from the book with the experiences and responses of the children, I created a final adventure for the class in which they became special agents with a mission to accomplish – the rescue of Nicobobinus. They were given a map covered in clues, information and problems to solve and worked in small groups as agents, deciding exactly how to rescue Nicobobinus. After several hours of brainstorming, discussion and detailed planning, each group achieved the task in many different ways and the agents then wrote individual accounts of their mission. Without exception, each one reflected a wealth of detail, knowledge and understanding that was only possible from their total involvement and commitment.

At the end of the project, parents were invited to school to share the breadth and depth of the many vivid learning experiences and curricular areas that had been covered. A grandmother spent considerable time admiring both the quality and quantity of work the children had produced, amazed that it had all started 'from only a book'. Only a book! That book had been our vessel on an exciting voyage of discovery, that stretched and challenged and changed each one of us far beyond the realms charted by Terry Jones.

Notes

1 J. Mark (1989) *Zeno was Here*, London: Pan.
2 R. Williams (1977) *Marxism and Literature*, Oxford: Oxford University Press.
3 DES (1988) *Report of the Committee of Inquiry into the Teaching of English* (Kingman Report), London: HMSO.
4 DES (1989) *English for Ages 5 to 16* (Cox Report), London: HMSO.
5 T. S. Eliot (1933) *The Use of Poetry and the Use of Criticism*, London: Faber and Faber.
6 J. Gardam (1986) *Kit in Boots*, London: Julia Macrae.
7 C. Dickens, (1971) *Our Mutual Friend*, edited Stephen Gill, London: Penguin (first published 1864–5).
8 H. Mayhew (1861) *London Labour and the London Poor*, London: Charles Griffin.
9 T. Jones (1985) *Nicobobinus*, London: Puffin.

Index